MADE TO
BE LOVED

Enjoying Spiritual Intimacy with God and Your Spouse

Steve and Valerie Bell

MOODY PRESS

CHICAGO

All Scripture quotations, unless indicated, are taken from the *Holy Bible: New International Version*®. NIV®. Copyright © 1973, 1978, 1984 by International Bible Society. Used by permission of Zondervan Publishing House. All rights reserved.

The "NIV" and "New International Version" trademarks are registered in the United States Patent and Trademark Office by International Bible Society. Use of either trademark requires permission of International Bible Society.

Scripture quotations marked (NLT) are taken from the *Holy Bible,* New Living Translation, copyright © 1996. Used by permission of Tyndale House Publishers, Inc., Wheaton, Illinois 60189. All rights reserved.

Scripture quotations marked (TLB) are taken from the *Living Bible* copyright © 1971. Used by permission of Tyndale House Publishers, Inc., Wheaton, Illinois 60189. All rights reserved.

Scripture quotations from *The Message* are copyright © by Eugene H. Peterson 1993, 1994, 1995. Used by permission of NavPress Publishing Group.

Scripture quotations marked (NASB) are taken from the *New American Standard Bible,* © 1960, 1962, 1963, 1968, 1971, 1972, 1973, 1975, 1977, and 1994 by The Lockman Foundation, La Habra, Calif. Used by permission.

Scripture quotations marked (KJV) are taken from the King James Version.

ISBN: 0-8024-3399-5

3 5 7 9 10 8 6 4 2

Printed in the United States of America

As we read Steve and Valerie's book, many faces come to mind of folks whose marriages could be helped, saved, and transformed by the Bells' realistic, deeply spiritual wisdom and do-able suggestions. Then *our* faces appear in our minds—this book is for us, too.

Made to Be Loved is honest, alive, and full of counsel that will actually make a difference. Our opinion? You really ought to read this book.

RACHAEL AND LARRY CRABB

Steve and Valerie have opened their hearts in a powerful way to help all of us move more closely to God and to each other. If authentic intimacy with our Lord and your spouse is what you long for, then this book is what you've been looking for.

MARTIE AND JOE STOWELL

To Brendan and Kailey Bell,
to celebrate your love and your marriage
on September 19, 1998.
May you always know that
you were made to be loved.

Contents

EXERCISES TO DEVELOP SPIRITUAL INTIMACY

Acknowledgments

A book is a team project. The names on the book's spine tell such an incomplete story about its creation. We would like to extend our thanks to two team members who helped us with this project.

Our thanks to Jim Bell, editorial director at Moody Press, for sharing with us the initial concept for the book. Thanks for your original thoughts and generous sharing of those ideas with us. Thank you also for trusting us to write on this topic that is one of your own passion areas.

Thanks also to Jim Vincent for editing this book with the great patience and passion for structure and detail that has helped organize *Made to Be Loved* into a coherent whole. Thank you for putting up with our peccadilloes! We appreciate you immensely.

Introduction

We saw them years ago in a window display of a store, and they have haunted us ever since. They were a beautiful man and woman. Cast in bronze by the sculptor, they eternally hold their pose. Longing etches their exquisitely rendered faces with hungry sadness. Wistfully the two lean across a bench towards each other, communicating a combined sense of longing and separation—yet they will remain forever unable to touch.

The artist has captured their conflicted feelings. They drink from each other's eyes, yet the stiffness of their bodies suggests distrust, fear, and disconnectedness. They hurt and hunger and long for each other without a way to close the gap.

The sculpting captures the sad predicament of many flesh and blood married lovers—always leaning, yet always frustrated, wanting more, yet unable to come closer.

Besides the obvious truth captured about lovers in this sculpture—that we can be extremely conflicted in our feelings about each other—there is a hint of something else as well. Just as the bronze lovers need the resources of their sculptor to remold them if they ever hope to close their intimacy gaps, so too do we need divine help. Like the bronzes, we can't help ourselves. We are as powerless as they. Cast in steel, hearts too vulnerable to be soft, forged by our human limitations, damaged and damaging, human lovers are chronically limited. Instructions to "sit closer, communicate more clearly, trust more," however helpfully meant, will not resolve our dilemmas. Technique is not enough. To have the kind of marriage most of us want requires more than better communication, more than resolving our conflicts, more than improving our sex lives, even more than the "tweakings" of the greatest marriage counselor.

The marriage most couples long for is attainable, but it will require an adjustment of nothing less than our hearts—a recasting, a rebirth, a spiritual realignment by God Himself.

Every marriage needs God. Human love must surrender to a higher spiritual love in order to bring God's resources into the relationship. Every couple needs to have their marriage "recast" by God. We all need spiritual intimacy, not only with our marriage partner, but with our God—the God who made us relational, emotional, complex spiritual beings.

But for most couples, accessing God in their marriage is anything but easy. For some couples even the subtitle of this book, *Enjoying Spiritual Intimacy with God and Your Spouse,* appears unattainable and idealistic. Just the concept of spiritual intimacy evokes times of struggling to pray with each other, failed attempts at making Scripture meaningful in shared devotions, and awkward times of trying to worship together. Why is it that spiritual intimacy seems so hard and unattainable? There are at least three reasons we want to highlight.

First, spiritual intimacy measures a marriage's health on many levels, and spouses in even slightly unhealthy marriages will find spiritual intimacy difficult to sustain. It is like the little bird that miners carry down into the deep coal shafts. As the oxygen thins out, the bird dies first, and then the miners know their own survival is at stake. The death of the bird alerts and alarms them. When there is trouble in a marriage, when a relationship is running out of "oxygen," the lack of spiritual intimacy is symptomatic. It reveals an unhealthy situation.

The last thing a couple want to do when they are carrying negative baggage with each other is to hold hands and pray, or join hearts together in worship. Couples experiencing trouble in their relationship may continue to live together—eat meals, pay their bills, raise the kids, even have sex and share other aspects of their lives—but will often draw the line by refusing to be "soulish" together. In a troubled marriage, spiritual intimacy is the first thing to go.

One revealing story of a troubled marriage from the Old Testament demonstrates how a disconnected spiritual intimacy sounds an alarm about serious problems ahead. Early in his reign Israel's King David brought the ark of God back to Jerusalem. In what can only be described as an extreme act of open, ecstatic worship, the king danced before God "with all his might" while clad in a linen ephod (an upper garment of the high priest). His wife, Michal (interestingly described in this text only as Saul's daughter—perhaps capturing her heart condition as much as her birth status), looked through a window and saw her husband's public religious display and "despised him in her heart" (2 Samuel 6:16). All the people celebrated that great day except one—Michal.

When David returned home, she met him and immediately attacked him verbally. "How the king of Israel has distinguished himself today, disrobing in the sight of the slave girls of his servants as any vulgar fellow would!" (verse 20). Most likely Michal's objection to David's public worship that day was not about public nudity (he undoubtedly remained dressed) but about removing the royal garments appropriate to his position in life.[1] She was married to a king, not a commoner, and she wanted him to behave as such.

But David countered her: "I will become even more undignified than this, and I will be humiliated in my own eyes. I will celebrate before the Lord. But by these slave girls you spoke of, I will be held in honor." And to that marriage clash Scripture adds this sad side note: "And Michal daughter of Saul had no children to the day of her death" (verses 22–23).

Was Michal put away? Was she cast from the marriage bed? It is difficult to know if the two incidents—the argument and the barrenness—were related. But if she was put away, doesn't that seem like a stiff reprisal for a wife who objected to her husband's public decorum? Look closer. Much more is tearing at this marriage than a wife's criticism.

Michal's refusal to worship with David, her disdain of his celebrative soul, her refusal to match him spiritually (letting any grateful tears stream down her face, smearing her makeup), her stiffening against abandoning herself to God with arms raised toward heaven and feet feeling the worship music, her lack of joy in her husband's spirituality, her distanced soul from him—all of these responses to her husband were more indicative of the break in their relationship than the actual, somewhat reasonable words she spoke that day. The miners' bird in the David and Michal marriage was on its last breath. The disconnectedness of their spiritual intimacy was sounding an alarm about the health of their marriage.

Like David and Michal, one reason couples struggle accessing God in their marriages is because they are moving into separateness, not connectedness in other areas of their lives. Christian couples need to pay attention to this critically important signal in their own marriages.

The second reason that experiencing spiritual intimacy with one's spouse is difficult may have more to do with our religious culture than our own marriage relationships. Within evangelical Christian circles spiritual intimacy is often narrowly defined in terms of techniques, methods, and how-tos. By primarily instructing couples on how to have "quiet times" together, inadvertently the focus has been more on the *means* while underplaying the most valuable *end*—a fulfilling relationship with God and each other. We suspect some couples will not even pick up this book because of their assumptions about its message. Most believers have repeatedly heard the definition of a successful spiritual life for couples as one in which there is a "quiet time" together—including participation in the basic traditional disciplines of prayer, Bible reading, and worship. Many couples dismiss any hope for spiritual intimacy, concluding the prescription for it sounds like "busy work," or the boring compulsories for Christian couples.

Couples struggle making these disciplines meaningful to such an extent that we have concluded the traditional "starting place" for spiritual intimacy—a devotional life together—assumes way too much about a couple's spiritual foundation and their basic understanding of God. Many husbands and wives are unable to apply spiritual truth.

So the second reason Christian couples commonly struggle with developing spiritual intimacy in their marriage is a limited definition that has focused more on methodology than relationship with God and each other. We believe that Christian couples will benefit from some creative thought about how to access God into their marriages. There are *many ways* for a husband and wife to access God and enjoy Him together as a married couple; this book will look at many of them.

You may wonder why we refer to the need to access God *into* our marriages; isn't God already *in* our lives? Yes, God entered our lives when we became His children through faith in Christ. Yet too often many couples function on a practical level as if He is on the periphery. As husbands and wives we must learn to access Him into the center of our relationship. That is the goal of this book, to help couples bring God into the center of their marriage.

A third reason couples struggle in their pursuit of spiritual intimacy is their natural resistance to change. Achieving genuine spiritual intimacy without an accompanying life change is impossible. Just going through the motions of "spiritual life"—while a marriage is strained by resentment, anger, selfishness, or distrust—is sure to produce a great deal of stress and marital discomfort. Nothing is more hypocritical or off-putting than spiritual forms without accompanying life change.

In a powerful and memorable scene from Robert Duvall's film, *The Apostle,* the unfaithful preacher/husband in a dying marriage begs his adulterous wife, "Pray with me. Just get down on your knees and pray with me." She refuses. The very thought of praying together as a "quick fix" is sickening to her and, she knows because of his unrepentant lifestyle, useless. Going through the motions of spiritual intimacy will not heal a sick or dying relationship. No formula approach to spirituality can substitute for real intimacy with God, an intimacy that changes each of us to the core of our beings. When God is "let into" or accessed into a marriage, a new awareness develops that enables us to see ourselves and our spouse very differently. That view, from God's eyes as it were, moves us very quickly, and sometimes quite dramatically, into life change.

The third reason, then, that many struggle with spiritual intimacy in their marriage is that most of us are resistant to change. Discovering and enjoying spiritual intimacy—authentic relationship with God and each other—requires ongoing growth, movement, and change.

Because a couple typically struggles in one (or more) of those three areas, our focus in this book is not primarily about a couple's "quiet time" but about "Christianizing" a marriage—developing an applied spirituality that welcomes God into all of life, including those most intimate moments of relating together. Chapters 4 through 11 highlight seven life-changing spiritual intimacy exercises that will help spouses learn to access God into their marriage. Our goal is to emphasize the *end result* of spiritual intimacy: an ongoing, satisfying relationship with God and each other.

Finally, we confess that up to this point we've resisted writing a book about marriage. What sane, God-fearing couple, knowing their own issues or problems, would presume to be marriage experts? However, like many couples we continue to learn from a gracious God; we have found help in developing and practicing the very spiritual intimacy exercises that appear on the following pages. We recommend them to you. We believe they are powerful and practical instruments of mutual attachment, joy, and understanding towards God.

It's our conviction that "marriageability" can be learned—that Christian couples have the greatest potential for the deepest human connecting, for the most accepting understanding, and for relational joy. Our hope is simple: Perhaps what has worked for us will work for others. We offer what we have learned from one very human (and sometimes struggling) couple to another.

Additionally, writing this book has required more public vulnerability about our own relationship than we are naturally inclined to share. What is more worthy of protection than the relationship between a husband and wife? Can any couple afford to be that honest and vulnerable about their marriage? When Jim Bell, editorial director at Moody Press (and no relation!), first approached us about doing this project, we were initially reluctant. *Good idea,* we thought, *but find some other Christian couple to write it.* But in time the appeal of the concept and our growing awareness of the obvious need overcame our reluctance.

So, how honest and vulnerable can we be about our marriage? That's the question we've asked ourselves as we've worked on this project. We want to be helpful without overloading you or overexposing the tangled "spaghetti" of our relationship. We are not any more comfortable "dancing in ephods"—shedding our "protective garments" of propriety and formality—than you might be reading about it.

Still, our marriage is the one we know best. It must serve as our model—both good and bad. Our memories in some ways appear like the afterimages on the eye, the images we see over the dark backdrop of our closed eyes—the remaining sunlight, the dancing patterns of color and form, images that are a little softer, a little blurred in detail, but visible even though the present is more clear and focused. Each chapter will introduce a metaphorical afterimage—a remembered highlight of our relationship that captures our spiritual development. The afterimages include letters to each other (or from our families), snatches of journal entries, inscriptions on wedding rings, and recalled conversations in passing that have stuck. They are the remembered images of a marriage, sometimes exquisite with joy and also grievously sorrowful. They remind us of great arguments; yet from the safer present we no longer feel the raging passion that fueled them. Afterimages stick and demand interpretation, and sometimes reinterpretation, in today's safer, more sane light.

We've struggled with that kind of vulnerability in writing this book, but we have concluded that today *is* a safe enough place for us to share about marriage. Laugh with us, feel with us, learn with us. We invite you to join us in the private recesses of our married hearts where our direction is towards a greater celebration of our God and of each other.

One final explanatory word. We realize that some may think us too "normal" to be an exciting read. Others may judge our marriage as one not "put through the fire," lacking details of great suffering which result from issues involving adultery, separation, divorce, alcoholism, suicide, abuse; or any other life horrors that afford "credibility." If you wonder, *What do they have to give us when we've suffered more?* we say that even though our life circumstances may look different at a glance, the principles of spiritual intimacy are the same for all marriages regardless of the specifics. We, with our readers, share the same God, if not the same life stories. We all are God's story. The experiences differ, but in a sense the plot is the same.

What is the plot? A man and woman want a great marriage. They try, but fail. God intervenes. Life is sweeter though much is still the same. It is a marriage miracle to those experiencing such rebirth, such recasting.

Join us as we explore together the recesses of God's great heart. By the time you read the last page, may the message that sticks with you be that you and your spouse were *made to be loved* and that your marriage is the vehicle God intends to use to bless you both.

Afterimage

"The first twenty-five years were the hardest. After that our arguing became less intense and less frequent. Just remember, the second twenty-five years are the best."

(Aunt Corda, speaking to Steve and Valerie during the celebration of her fiftieth wedding anniversary)

1

What Makes a Marriage Successful?

*O*n this particular evening we are dining with some new acquaintances in south Florida. The night is tropical, balmy, and our table conversation becomes relaxed and informal long before dessert has been served.

"So . . ." our host casually remarks as he leans back against his chair, his body language open—an ankle perched on his knee, one hand clinking ice cubes in his swirling glass, the other resting around the back of his date's chair—"how long have you two been married?"

We knew it was coming. When we are talking to other people, eventually, it seems, they get around to asking us "the question." *Where is it written,* we wonder, *that we must always answer this one? The "So, how long have you been married?" question.*

"Twenty-eight years," Steve replies.

"Twenty-eight years! That's amazing! Congratulations!" these table friends blurt out almost in unison.

We receive their reaction with smiles and thank yous, but inside each of us is silently cringing. Both of us have traveled this path many times. We know some of the assumptions our dining friends are making about us at this moment. We understand some of the misconceptions about long marriages they are "chewing on" as we speak.

"That's what I'm looking for," the character at the end of the table announces. His voice drips with sarcasm: "I'm looking for the right woman, next time."

Good luck, Romeo! we're thinking. Our social smiles hold back an honest response to his declaration, remembering that this casual social setting begs for a light touch, not a treatise on long marriages. We suspect none of our questioners *really* wants to hear how we've arrived at twenty-eight years together. Anyway, how could we tell them the truth we have learned in this marriage of such a long duration? ("Long" by this culture's standards, anyway.) It's like they're saying to us, "Congratulations! Here's to the couples who do not divorce, or worse—murder each other! Here's to long-haul marriages!" In North America, where the average duration of a marriage is just over nine years,[1] let it be known that you've been married ten, eighteen, or thirty-eight years and you'll probably get a round of applause. Twenty-eight continuous years together must mean a couple is having a successful marriage. A typical assumption: *Lucky couple! They each found the "right" partner and the rest has been easy.*

We consider "Romeo" seated across from us. It's apparent he's thinking that there is one right person out there who is perfect for him, and probably problem-free. He just has to locate her. Simply find the "right" person and then you can expect a successful marriage. These new friends want to believe that about us. They want our enduring marriage to support their belief in the culturally cherished fantasy about relationships.

What we want to tell them (and what we sense they really don't want to hear) is that we were not just lucky! Nor has our marriage been easy. Actually, good marriages are rarely easy, but more often the result of hard work. Furthermore, even good marriages can be bad sometimes—and painful.

HONEST WORDS ABOUT MARRIAGE

This Romeo at our table should have had the talk we had years ago with Valerie's Great-Aunt Corda. Our extended family was celebrating Aunt Corda and Uncle Jeff's fiftieth wedding anniversary in California. We were newlyweds. That evening Corda took us aside and confided, "The first twenty-five years were the hardest. After that our arguing became less intense and less frequent. Just remember, the second twenty-five years are the best."

The Best Comes Later

Aunt Corda's words were prophetic. Our marriage is like the wine served at the Galilean wedding in Cana (see John 2:1–10). The best wine (which was only water until Jesus got involved) was served near the end. The best part of our marriage also began after Jesus changed us, leading us toward greater spiritual intimacy in our marriage. For us, the best has come more toward these later years of our relationship, as we've come closer to God (and thus closer to each other's souls).

What we want to say to Romeo and other romantics like him: A successful marriage may not be what you perceive it to be at present. No one experiences the marriage he hoped for just by finding the "right" person. There is no such thing as a marriage lottery where a few "lucky" couples end up winning big and everyone else loses. Although marriage could be considered the ultimate risk, what unfolds in real life is much more about investment than chance.

The Cost Is Great

Consider the perils of marriage. On the strength of a fragile promise before family and friends two individuals close their future options and escape routes and vow to "be there" for each other forever, no matter what the personal price. People like you, like us—who are too sane to risk life and limbs on extreme sports or gamble away hard-earned savings in casinos—still willingly risk their future happiness on the perilous possibilities of love.

The wedding symbols abound with romance: flowers, ribbons, white lace, frothy icing lavished over towering wedding cakes, and stringed quartets playing Mozart. They suggest only idyllic before-the-Fall, Garden-of-Eden-like days to come. The potential personal cost of these magnanimous lifetime pledges is rarely addressed in any wedding ceremony.

George Bernard Shaw noted one great irony about the wedding ceremony: "When two people are under the influence of the most violent, most insane, most delusive, and most transient of passions, they are required to swear that they will remain in that excited, abnormal, and exhausting condition continuously until death do them part."[2]

This enormous gap between wedding symbolism and marriage reality sometimes makes the two of us wonder, *What do weddings have to do with actual marriages anyway?* We need truer marriage symbols on the wedding day. Perhaps society should require couples, clad in army fatigues and combat boots, to bungee jump to their places in front of the minister. Ushers should then be allowed to roam the aisles with microphones to publicly interview crying wedding guests to discover the *real* reason for their tears. And if we really want the symbolic to reflect reality, then a great new tradition would be that the bride and groom demonstrate their ability to synchronize swim in a baptistery stocked with piranha, while a soloist sings "You Don't Bring Me Flowers Anymore."

But why be that honest? Brides and grooms will eventually learn the truth, the voice of romance protests. *And besides, why scare them off? Only a mere few would get married if weddings were that baldly realistic!*

And perhaps there's a kindness in that thinking, but after twenty-eight years of marriage and twenty-five years of full-time ministry, including counseling and marrying more couples than we've kept count of, we suspect that even the baldest symbolic truth would not deter most couples in love from marrying. The prevailing attitude seems to be that *newlyweds will learn the truth about marriage soon enough. In the meantime let them enjoy the honeymoon.*

Let's be realistic. Would most brides and grooms even be open to a more honest approach early on? After all, no one is more hopelessly hopeful or apt to think that the relational laws of gravity do not apply to them than couples who are in love. Most couples in love think like we thought before the wedding. *We're special, not like everyone else. In the history of mankind, no one has ever been this in love. We are a match made in heaven, pulled together by some great magnetic force, perfectly paired. We are twin souls, whose spirits throb as one heartbeat.*

OUR PERSONAL REVELATION

Ah, Youth!

We were young, ages twenty and twenty-one, when we married as college students. Endorphins flowed, hormones raged, and, in our thinking, signs pointed to an effortlessly agreeable, tension-free marriage. We were not so naive to expect life together to be perfect; but honestly, we thought "ideal" was within reach. During our dating years and courtship we had intentionally discussed every subject imaginable pertaining to life, yet never had an argument. We seemed to be in complete agreement in our outlook. Life was sweet.

Looking back there were other signs, but at the time they seemed insignificant compared to the looming, wonderful possibilities that were unfolding for us. Early in our dating relationship I had been impressed with Steve's ability to care for me. My parents were wonderful in many areas, but their laissez-faire approach to life resulted in overlooking some details of their children's lives. Additionally, money was scarce. We all made do. It was considered a resourceful trait in the Burton household to learn to do without. Coats often lacked accompanying gloves and scarves. Shoes were always the most basic of colors. I was hesitant to ask my parents for anything beyond what was absolutely needed.

Enter Steve. Without knowing about these gaps in my childhood, and with apparent ease, he began attending to the physical details of my life. I had never met a young man with such organizational skills or ability to juggle details. He showed an amazing capacity for hard work and earning money. All of this he showered on me. He had a great life force and incredible energy, requiring only four or five hours of sleep a night.

For the first time, someone was ordering my disorder. Nothing seemed to matter more to him than me, and he demonstrated that by giving even the smallest matters involving me his focused attention. Little by little life started to change. Thanks to Steve's generosity, I had supplies of panty hose in various colors, instead of one patched-up, all-purpose pair. He made sure I was never without change for the phone or money for shampoo. He supervised my class schedule, arranging for the best teachers and best class times. Here was a luxury— I didn't have to stuff cold hands into coat pockets to stay warm; my coats now had matching mittens or gloves. He also made sure that I wore them. I didn't have to do without, or even ask. With an ability far beyond his age, he cared for me. This was a kind of seduction I had never experienced with anyone before!

We were both aware of what we stood to gain in relationship to each other. Steve felt the same magic. "Valerie brought flair to my order, soul to my function, creativity to the myriad details of my life. Whereas she says I brought her incredible care, energy, order, and joy, I found she gave me a new, spontaneous edge, a focused purpose to my make-something-good-happen approach to life and relationships."

Reality Sets in: Opposing Forces

Neither of us had any idea that there might be a downside or personal cost in being married to each other. In the years that followed, time, that great teacher, would reveal the truth about our relationship. Not only were we not twin souls, we were not sibling souls; our souls were not even distantly related! Unconsciously we had married not so much because of similarities but for our differences. In many areas, we were each other's opposites.

It didn't take very long after the wedding for us to realize we were no longer the picture of *joie de vivre*. The anticipated utopia, the effortless closeness, the exquisite permeating sweetness of the Garden of Eden seemed like a lost piece of our naive history. Real life didn't seem to have much in common with the "Garden" anymore.

The very traits that had initially attracted us were developing the power to repel. Magnetic forces became opposing forces. My insistence on attention to details increasingly felt like overbearing control to Valerie. What had previously been considered a wonderful ability now seemed like a ridiculous passion for the piddly. And on the flip side, while I was still drawn to Valerie's free-spirited, spontaneous love of life, I began seriously wondering, *Will she ever get her act together? Go-with-the-flow was fine and loads of fun in our courtship days, but is everyday life like this even sustainable? Can I handle it over the long haul?*

We had our first arguments. We experienced anger with more intensity than we had ever felt in our lives. And fear: We were haunted with unspoken thoughts too frightening to bring into the light. *Was this marriage a mistake? Did I marry the "wrong" person?* We spent lots of energy in those initial years trying to recreate each other into our own particular images. But without success.

THE END OF YOUNG LOVE

What was happening between us—or not happening!—was taking its toll. How we wish someone had told us that much of what we were going through is a normal, though grievous, loss of youthful love—a loss, we believe, that is experienced by most couples. Our human love, we sadly realized, would not be enough to fulfill, satisfy, and care for each other in the days ahead. We were like the sculpted pair in the introduction of this book: wanting more from our relationship, leaning and straining toward each other, but unable to close the ever-widening intimacy gap on our own.

Not Giving Up in the Midst of Pain

A marriage at this relational impasse can be loaded with pain, so much pain that some couples refuse to examine truthfully where their relationship stands. They surrender their hopes for a fulfilling marriage, settling for a dull coexistence or a mere mutual toleration. But for couples who have the courage not to give up on their relationship, who maintain the conviction that life together could be more meaningful, this passage can become not an impasse, but a door through which there is the potential for a more honest and healthy intimate relationship—a love based on reality, not fantasy.

C. S. Lewis was realistic about the pain involved in the loss of romantic love, but he was also positive about the potential gain it presents to couples. He viewed this loss as a necessary step to achieving mature love. "I believe it [youthful love] must *always* be lost in some way: every merely natural love has to be crucified before it can achieve resurrection," he wrote. "Happy *old* couples have come through a difficult death and re-birth. But far more have missed the re-birth."[3]

Perhaps that was what Great-Aunt Corda was trying to tell us. If someone had just spelled that out more clearly early on! We thought that only "bad" marriages experienced such relational bankruptcy.

Within that very first year of married life, something between us had changed, had been lost, had maybe even died. We would never divorce. That was a given. But at what an enormous personal price we stayed together!

Marriage can cost a person more than any other single investment in life. There is so little return on the promises to stay together when a marriage is at this stage. Life that was meant to be celebrated in relationship together becomes a practice in enduring. For the investment of your entire lifetime, too often the return is meager affection overshadowed by disillusionment and disappointment. No one who is truly honest would blame someone in this kind of marriage for sometimes thinking, *There has to be more!*

Perhaps that is your unspoken thought. It certainly was ours back in those early days. In our own ways we longed for a closer coming together, a way of melding our differences. We ached for intimacy and the return of our innocence. We wanted what we had experienced before. In spite of the ongoing struggle, which persisted with tremendous intensity at times, we each held to a conviction that we had been made to be loved. Something inside us refused to let go of that hope for meaningful intimacy.

The Benefits of a Long Look Back

With a long look back, we remember major arguments marked by great intensity and heated verbal exchanges. Like any other couple, we had the potential to turn our marriage celebration from wine into blood. For us, however, bloodletting or physical battering was only figurative; but unforgettable afterimages of anger in our memories certainly qualified us to heed the scriptural admonition, "Beware of ruining each other" (Galatians 5:15 TLB).

The present is safe enough to examine and expose the truth about the past. We agree with Great-Aunt Corda—the latter part of our marriage has been so much better than the beginning. We have learned not just to understand or tolerate our differences, but literally to honor and celebrate the diversity of our personalities that make up this unique union. We know we need each other precisely because we are not alike. Through these years together we have gained the understanding that this marriage was part of a divine plan, a spiritual meshing, a needed alliance, which when seen through God's eyes makes sense, even when we ourselves still occasionally experience the painful "rub" of just how different we are.

With a long look backward, we can now see that Jesus has performed the miracle at the marriage of Cana over and over again for us. He has taken our watered-down marriage, with its disappointments, frustrations, sadness, dullness . . . and miraculously, spiritually re-birthed it into marriage wine! It's sweeter. More caring. More understanding. There is grace for each other's shortcomings and minor offenses. We are a resurrected, rebirthed version of the young people who began this journey of commitment together.

"But," you may be protesting, "what if we've tried being spiritually intimate without success? Honestly, we struggle to get much out of Bible reading, or to see it translating into our relationship in any meaningful way. Prayer between us is so awkward. Spiritual intimacy just doesn't seem to work for us."

Then, good news! This book is for you. There are many ways to access God into a marriage. Defining spiritual intimacy in marriage as a couple having a structured devotional life is too narrow an interpretation. Experiencing a "quiet time" as a couple is just one of the avenues to God—a means, not the end. Often a couple needs some additional spiritual groundwork laid before they can be very successful in studying, praying, or worshiping together. That is the purpose of the spiritual intimacy exercises described in this book. Most couples, including many we know in ministry, need to build a foundation for spiritual intimacy before they can move very far with traditional prayer and quiet times together.

Our desire is not to further weigh down anyone with frustration or a sense of failure about methodologies. Our hope is that we may facilitate your letting go of any guilt you may feel about the lack in quality of spiritual intimacy between you and your spouse. Guilt shames us away from God. Instead, we want to help you rediscover the relational delight, joy, and great comfort of His love for both you and your spouse. The goal, the desired result of spiritual intimacy with each other and God, is a mutual flight of dependence into God's arms and His love.

Will this work for you? What is your alternative? Most marriages have become too accomplished at adapting to hopelessness. It's harder to hope. It takes humility to admit to wanting more. It takes courage to believe that the longings of your heart are possible. Whatever the discouragement, know this: Even though a couple may not be "soul mates"— that is, similar in all or most ways—they can still be profoundly connected when both are mating their souls to God.

This book is for married partners who want more, who experience unfilled longing in their marriages. If you've ever felt so lonely and isolated it was physically painful; if you've ever cried out to God the exasperated cry of Eden, "This woman [or this man] you have given me!"; if sex has become mechanical, if conversation is formulaic, if relationship is all but gone, if the spark has died—you are in a good position. You are ready for God to show up in your marriage. You are ready to turn wedding water into marriage wine.

Afterimage

November 11, 1968

Honey (yes, <u>you</u>!—I can call you that now, can't I?)
Three things:
1. I love you!
2. Today you paid me the most beautiful compliment a girl can ever receive. Yes, yes, I'll marry you! But I don't deserve you. Thank you for the carefully considered and prayerfully thought-out way you proposed. I know our love has room to grow, although I can't imagine now where it will expand—it seems so big now. Anyway, we have a year and a half to learn and grow before you acquire a little wife and <u>all</u> my bills. (That library fine ought to be pretty impressive by then!)
3. I want to take advantage of this time God has given us to the fullest extent. That means to enjoy each day together, not to throw this waiting time away as insignificant. I want to grow to be an asset to your life—a person to encourage and love you, a pal, a sweetheart, your biggest fan and unreserved lover. Let's not grow impatient but increasingly happy for all the memories we'll make during this part of our lives. I hope we go broke buying scrapbooks and albums.
I am so happy!

> *Much love,*
> *Val*

(Excerpted from a letter written the day Steve officially proposed)

2

Made
to
Be
Loved

A young friend of our family said it best the other day. After an extremely difficult first year of marriage, after months of counseling and trying to get to the root of their anger, after giving and receiving woundedness upon woundedness, her husband and she had begun to see some improvement in their relationship. They were encouraged. They had also come to a decision.

"Now that we have agreed not to get a divorce, we want to try to make our marriage as good as it can be," she said.

Our thoughts exactly! A successful marriage is one that is in process of becoming "as good as it can be." Our young friends had expressed one of the most important turning points a marriage can take, the beginning of rebirth, the desire to do the work to make your marriage "as good as it can be." A successful marriage cannot simply be measured by how long a couple has stayed together. A successful marriage is about the direction the relationship is heading. And this direction must be moving towards *intimacy*—a spiritual intimacy between the couple and God, and a soul intimacy between the husband and wife. Such intimacy creates a greater connectedness and genuineness for the couple, and a greater care for each other.

GOING BEYOND HUMAN INTIMACY

Here is an important underlying principle: Marriage will never be its most excellent version of itself if it is established with the building blocks of human intimacy alone. Marriages built on human love and human intimacy are like the houses two of the three little pigs built: They may appear sturdy, but as time passes and with the cumulative piling of life's circumstances, they often do not withstand the huffs and puffs or weightiness of adversity. Successful marriages—marriages that are becoming as good as they can be—involve couples who are moving towards God and each other. The couple together is moving from mere human intimacy toward a deeper, more fulfilling spiritual intimacy.

Spiritual intimacy has the potential of improving any marriage, no matter how far the direction has been away from God or each other. Christian couples have the potential to have the deepest relating, the closest connecting, the most sympathetic understanding, and the sweetest lovemaking. It's all available to us, if we will tap into it. Spiritual intimacy is what we would have liked to have talked about with our dining friends in Florida. It has been our journey towards God— not luck, not finding or being the right soul mate for each other—that has rebirthed us. It has been God's involvement in our marriage that has accounted for the growing satisfaction and enduring relationship we're now enjoying.

Understanding Spiritual Intimacy

What exactly do we mean by spiritual intimacy? Here's our definition of this crucial element of successful marriages: *Spiritual intimacy is the satisfying connectedness that occurs when a husband and wife learn to access God and experience Him together on the deepest levels.*

Moving towards spiritual intimacy certainly includes the traditional disciplines of Bible study and prayer; but it is much more than methods, daily checklists, acquiring biblical knowledge, or accounting for how much time you spend praying with each other. Discovering spiritual intimacy together begins with the understanding in your deepest being that God has created you for relationship with Him. You were made to be loved. And God wants to bless your marriage as a primary vehicle through which you would experience that love. It's how He designed marriage to work.

The Benefits of Spiritual Intimacy

Achieving spiritual intimacy has multiple benefits. Here are several of them:

- Spiritual intimacy nurtures a safe environment for optimal growth as individuals and as a couple.
- Spiritual intimacy accesses all of God's healing resources of love, grace, and forgiveness into a marriage.
- Spiritual intimacy invites God into a home and restores some of the Garden of Eden's before-the-Fall joy and comfort that mankind once experienced in God's presence.
- Spiritual intimacy alters a husband or wife's perspective about the other and introduces into the relational dynamic all of God's creative problem-solving genius.
- Spiritual intimacy redirects us appropriately towards God as our greatest love and the One most able to meet needs. It releases couples from unrealistic expectations about being "perfectly" matched.
- Spiritual intimacy ensures the formation of a three-way alliance: with God and each other. This strengthens the couple as they stand together in the inevitable storms of life.
- Spiritual intimacy restores our marriage relationship as it moves us gently toward God and each other. *Everything* is better. Relationship with God allows us to experience the previously hidden layers of intimacy in our marriage. The potential for the best and most fulfilling sex lives belongs to Christian couples alone. The potential for the best family life possible belongs exclusively to Christ-honoring believers.
- Spiritual intimacy brings us into a higher level of relating to each other. We become each other's ministers and the primary relationship that blesses each other's existence.

Intimacy Without Christ?

"But, isn't it possible for couples to be intimate without Christ?" a Christian husband asked us recently on this point. "I'm aware of a lot of secular marriages that seem to work—at least appear to be close, devoted, and loyal."

True, we respond, but we must not mistake a deep human love for spiritual intimacy. Valerie's human love, captured in her letter to Steve after he proposed (see the afterimage, page 28), could deepen over time, but it would not automatically lead to spiritual intimacy with him. Without a commitment to and partnership with God, without a deep loving relationship with Him that receives and gives back, God's divine agape love will not be possible in marriage. The resources of divine mercy and grace go untapped in the relationship of a man and woman who have not included God in their marriage. Spiritual intimacy between a human couple and God moves the love to a higher plane than even the most fulfilling human loves.

The move toward making a marriage optimal, not simply good, is by definition a move toward God. It is a decision to "Christianize" not only each spouse's individual life in relationship to God, but also the marriage relationship. Spiritual intimacy invites God's supernatural resources into a marriage that has previously been defined only by human limitation.

Conclusion? Even a seemingly great marriage will be enriched through the pursuit of spiritual intimacy. There are no authentic spiritually intimate couples without Christ included in the equation. Good human relationships may exist in a marriage, but we're talking about something more. Something better!

THE TRANSITION TO A REBIRTH

Some Pain

A rebirthed marriage is wonderful, but the birthing process may be messy. This book is intended to move you into that phase, or if you are already there, to help you define where your relationship stands, and then deliver you through the birth canal into new life with each other. But a warning is appropriate. The first stage of labor, after young love has faded and before a new vision for the relationship is cast, can be very painful.

Transition, the most intense stage of physical birthing, is also the most painful stage of marriage. This time in a marriage is often the most confusing, the most explosive, the most brutally honest. Experiencing a rebirthing process can feel like the worst period in a married couple's relationship. The symptoms won't seem very appealing, but a spiritually tuned-in couple will begin to understand that experiencing them is key to finding God's great resources of love for them, and, in turn, their most excellent love for each another.

Much Gain

Paradoxically, this transitional stage can be the beginning of greater health, of more honest relating, of actually forming the kind of marriage that is longed for so deeply. God wants to use this transitional stage to move us into deeper relationship with Him and greater marriageability to each other. And so, it's absolutely essential to measure the success and health of a marriage, not by its lack of emotional pain, but by its overall direction. Some of the dullest and deadest marriages are also the least painful.

For some couples, the painful symptoms of transition will characterize their relationship for the rest of their union. It's as if they never pass through the birth canal but stay stuck in the painful rebirthing period forever. For couples who fail to address their issues, this transitional phase will likely mark the beginning of the death of their relationship, where they live essentially separate lives though under the same roof. Understand, the relationship is dead, even if they manage to stay together for twenty-eight, thirty-eight, or forty-eight years!

But for others, those married couples who will, in time, achieve happy-old-couple status, this transitional stage is simply the irritating sand in the oyster that eventually creates the pearl. It will be the beginning of something new and rewarding.

HOW TO MAKE THE TRANSITION

How does a couple manage this difficult time in their relationship? How can a couple move through the pain of transition to greater health? The need for help to change is recognized by many who write and speak to those in difficult marriages. Achieving greater intimacy seems to be the common goal of the various prescribed solutions. In describing the dynamics of intimacy, even the experts have differing perspectives. Some label *fear* the great enemy of intimacy. That makes sense. But then along comes someone else who sees *anger* as the biggest barrier to intimacy. Others argue that *a lack of trust* hinders intimacy.

Who's right?

These factors are all pieces of the truth, but none reveals to us the complete picture. Trying to achieve intimacy in marriage by making a few adjustments here and there is like trying to learn to drive a car by mastering the specifics of all the mechanics. Tinker with the engine all you want, tweak and tune to the most exacting detail, align the tires, change the oil, and adjust the fluid levels—all important details—but unless you turn on the engine and put it in drive, you won't actually experience driving a car.

You can work long and hard at controlling your anger, or building trust, or overcoming fear, or enhancing your communication techniques. You can attend counseling sessions to expose all the nitty-gritty about the intimacy avoidance problems in your marriage. You can even master the language of *dysfunctionality* and *codependency,* coming to greater understanding, and still not be able to make the marriage work. Just as it's necessary to have a grasp of more than the mechanics to learn to drive a car, marriage must also be understood from the bigger perspective in order to make it work. A car is not intended just for mechanical tinkering and stationary tuning, but for driving.

The Goal: Made to Be Loved

The big picture about marriage involves more than relational "tweaking." Marriage is intended for more than a couple experiencing excellent communication, trust, or emotional safety with each other. The very essence of marriage is about spiritual intimacy—with God and with each other. Just as a car was made to be driven, we were made to be loved. When we marry, the new husband-wife relationship becomes a vehicle that God intends to help us experience and understand His love. Marriage is about spiritual intimacy. Spiritual intimacy brings a couple into the most satisfying connectedness and deepest levels of mutual relating and caring. A spiritually optimal marriage is an earthly picture of God's divine love.

But we cannot achieve this optimal state without God. Factor God out of marriage, and life together will be reduced to a tinkering of relational mechanics, a tweaking of assorted techniques, a tuning of understanding and expectations, instead of the dynamic, organic spiritual union it was intended to be. Without God in the equation, a marriage can only go so far. If it "sits in the driveway" year after year, never operating within the spiritual dimension, it's only a matter of time before a level of dissatisfaction sets in. Something deep inside us cries out to be fulfilled, wanting more of our marriage than what we "normally" experience.

That's because deep inside the core of our being we know we were made to be loved, not just adjusted to, or compensated for, or psychologically accommodated.

The Solution: Marriages "in Tune" with God

"But our marriage has so many problems" we can hear some readers saying. "Shouldn't we just deal with those issues first?" Yes, you may work on those issues; but realize that if you focus on trying to develop a "perfect" relationship by "fixing" your marriage or "fixing" each other, you may never get around to the ultimate goal of spirituality in the marriage. Your energy and attention could be diverted from God and toward the impossible goal of complete happiness in the relationship.

Yet with God, even a marriage of extremely disparate individuals can take on a spiritual dimension that fosters closeness and profound connecting, regardless of the unresolved issues. In other words, just as a car can still be driven though the tires aren't exactly aligned, or the engine isn't perfectly tuned, or the windshield wipers aren't operating in sync, a marriage can still be intimately connected even if husband and wife are not a "perfect" pair, have unresolvable personality differences, or face some other marriage misunderstanding. Realize that your "marriage machine" can still operate effectively when you are in tune with God.

THE ROLE OF COUNSELING

The marriages we know that have been reborn are those that have come to experience spiritual intimacy and healing. Sometimes healing came over a period of time directly through the spiritual dimension without counseling. And other times professional counseling served as the catalyst for couples becoming "as good as they can be." We do recommend counseling. It has been tremendously helpful in many lives. But we recommend it with the warning that from the very outset it's essential for each spouse to have realistic expectations for the experience.

The Benefits . . . and the Limits

The benefits of counseling are multiple: Counseling sessions can be extremely helpful in providing a language for discussion, in exposing the truth, in exploring what lies beneath the surface of the real issues in question, in bringing an outside, emotionally disengaged, educated voice to the confusion . . . to name a few. But if counseling fails to introduce the spiritual dimension, the end result may be only an "understanding toleration"—that is, a tinkering of mechanics, a tweaking of technique, instead of a heart change that realigns a couple to genuinely experience God together.

Can Christian counseling move a couple into spiritual intimacy? Sometimes. Hopefully, effective counseling will produce a heart change, or at least some movement towards grace with each other and obedient love of God. But don't *assume* that marriage counseling will necessarily move a couple closer toward God or each other.

Larry Crabb warns about the subtle values in some kinds of counseling.

> In the last decade or so, we have dignified the shallow appeal of "be happy, feel good" by substituting the more Christian-sounding invitation to find "a fulfilling life" and to become "self-actualized." . . . "Fulfillment" has taken on a greater urgency and value than "obedience." Psychologists do great damage by encouraging this reversal of priorities.
>
> Does fulfillment have a place in biblical thinking? Of course. Each of us has a deep concern for our own well-being, and this is as it should be. . . . The crucial issue is not whether we should be interested in our own welfare, but rather how we believe our welfare is best served. Pursuing whatever path brings the deepest immediate sense of internal well-being appears to be a rather sensible strategy for finding fulfillment. But the Bible teaches that there is a way which—although it *seems* right to a man—in the end leads to death: the tragedy of personal emptiness and desolation. Scriptures about dying to self, finding one's life by losing it, being crucified with Christ, and living only for Christ make it clear that realizing true fulfillment depends, not on preoccupation with fulfillment, but preoccupation with knowing God through absolute surrender.[1]

A marriage will fail to be truly spiritually intimate if it moves in the direction of self. A successful marriage moves in the direction of obedience and relational surrender to God and increased relationship with the marriage partner.

Counseling, when its primary goal is to eliminate pain, can do serious spiritual harm sending a spouse away from intimacy. Thus it may eventually destroy a marriage. Another psychologist, Dan Allender, warns about the danger of setting boundaries (when untempered by Christian principles) in order to eliminate personal pain.

> The setting of boundaries to prevent possible use and abuse often leads to self-centered, arrogant, autonomous self-protection. I talked to a

woman who had been immersed for years in a secular approach to boundary building. Her mother is an evil, hard, critical woman who would rather destroy her daughter than admit that her husband had abused the girl. For years, the daughter had set appropriate boundaries and "took care of herself." . . . She was transformed from a weak-kneed wimp to an angry, tough wench. And that was called progress.

Love has boundaries . . . but suffering is equally necessary for us because it strips away the pretense that life is reasonable and good, a pretense that keeps us looking in all the wrong places for the satisfaction of our souls.[2]

Recognizing Our Dependency on God

The ultimate goal of counseling should be to help us recognize our need for God and to run to Him. Psychological techniques can help strip our masks of self-sufficiency and probe beneath the surface, and at their finest, point out our utter dependence upon God. But counseling does have a tendency to divert people's pain into mere "tweaking" approaches—focusing on communication skills, boundary setting, or self-absorbed analysis—all of which may give us a sense of power again but likely will distract us from our need to depend on God. Psychological tweaking typically gets in the way if it factors God out of the healing process. Any "tweaking" that numbs the pain, any adjustment that moves us to feeling more powerful and self-reliant, any marriage theory that does not ultimately drive us into the arms of God is a dangerous diversion from the suffering that is a call to God Himself.

Jesus addressed this issue of power—derived from any area of self-sufficiency—that can keep us from recognizing our total dependency upon God.

Jesus looked around and said to his disciples, "How hard it is for the rich to enter the kingdom of God!"

The disciples were amazed at his words. But Jesus said again, "Children, how hard it is to enter the kingdom of God! It is easier for a camel to go through the eye of a needle than for a rich man to enter the kingdom of God." (Mark 10:23–24)

The rich man's wealth masked his sense of need for God and gave him a sense of power and self-sufficiency. The principle behind this passage is that any sense of personal power—any overconfidence we hold in our own abilities, talents, intelligence, skills, and insights learned through counseling, whatever—can be barriers that keep us from recognizing our utter dependency upon God, thereby numbing our pain and stopping our flight to Him.

Pursuing a spiritually intimate relationship with a spouse means to humble our self-reliance and psychological pride or tendency to divert and tweak. Instead, in utter dependence, stripped down to ephods and naked-souled, we must run to God!

INTRODUCING SPIRITUAL TRUTH INTO YOUR MARRIAGE

For a marriage to reach its full potential, at some point the truth about our utter dependence upon God must be introduced into the relationship. One or both spouses can begin this process. This is critically important. The spiritual lights can go on in one or both partners. A husband or wife alone, with a new spiritual perspective, can have a huge impact on the eventual success of the marriage. Just one mate moving towards God and away from self may be enough to affect the outcome of a marriage headed for trouble.

This raises another important issue about spiritual intimacy. Can a marriage become spiritually intimate if only one partner introduces God into the relationship? Our answer may surprise you: a qualified no. Why qualified? Because one partner, opening the door for God to enter the marriage, can begin the marriage's spiritual healing process. Scripture says, "A cord of three strands is not quickly broken" (Ecclesiastes 4:12), which can be interpreted to mean that the ultimate strong position in a marriage is for both partners to be "bound" to God together. But it's our conviction that even one spiritually tuned-in partner can introduce a meaningful spiritual dimension into a relationship. By definition it's not the ultimate, but in actuality even one spouse moving more towards God and away from self may begin the process of bringing God's greater involvement into the marriage.

LIFE'S GREATEST RESOURCE

Spiritual intimacy—the satisfying connectedness that occurs when a husband and wife learn to worship and experience God together on the deepest levels—is the greatest resource in marriage that we know. It's also the most untapped resource for marital fulfillment. Of all the challenges facing Christian marriages today, it's our belief that overlooking spiritual intimacy (and replacing it primarily with a psychological approach) is by far the greatest danger. How far the pendulum has swung! The problem is *not* psychology, but the typical expectations of what psychology can achieve.

These days it seems we expect so much from psychology, and so little from God!

Treating symptoms alone rarely deals with the causative disease. It's our observation that what's often presented as a "marriage issue" is more typically a spiritual problem that is negatively affecting the marriage.

Spiritual intimacy, or a marriage relationship where God is factored in, is marriage's most powerful resource for close, profound understanding and deep connecting. In a sense, spiritually intimate couples form an alliance with the very creator of marriage Himself! This union is life's most challenging and creative endeavor—a living art, a workmanship of His own making, requiring His direct involvement.

Think of it. How surprising it would be to hear about a married couple who never had sexual relations with each other; one would have reason to be alarmed that something so important was missing from their marriage.

If a married couple lived together, but kept their financial resources from each other, we would be right to wonder if they knew much about shared life.

If after the wedding a couple chose to live in separate homes or cities, instead of together, most of us would be surprised at such an arrangement.

Yet married couples live together all the time without sharing authentic spiritual life with each other. Even in many "Christian homes," there is very little prayer together or alone. Praise and delight of God are nearly foreign concepts. There is minimal expressed gratitude for each other. Seldom is there an openness to solutions beyond human, rational reasoning. Why aren't we equally disturbed by such relational omissions? Instead we are almost always surprised when we learn of the poverty of another relationship. *What? They're getting divorced? But they seemed like such a happy couple!*

Maybe you have been trying to improve your relationship, but have you considered that you can't have the "Garden" if God isn't there?

It's amazing. Nearly every facet of married life improves when there is spiritual intimacy between a couple and God. Here's a paradox: Even if everything stays the same—the issues, the personalities, the problems—everything can still be drastically changed. When adding the *spiritual* dimension we begin to see each other through softer lenses. Vulnerability seems safer, and before too long all other areas of intimacy improve. Through a spiritual perspective there is grace for each other, ministry for each other, care for each other's woundedness, instead of just those persistent unrealistic romantic expectations!

Yes, a couple who is spiritually intimate will discover that *everything* gets better. Communication does improve, sexuality takes on another dimension, and grace substitutes acceptance and understanding for the drive to change your spouse. What previously drove you crazy about your mate now drives you to laughter. And some of those irritating quirks may begin to take on a charm of their own. OK, maybe now we're pushing it! But truthfully, even arguing gets better. In time, the classic spiritual disciplines of the devotional life become less difficult and more attractive.

After a rough first year, or a difficult five years, or an impossible twenty-five years, a marriage can feel hopeless. It is. Humanly hopeless. But the resources of God's creative forces are waiting to be unleashed in the dynamics of the most hopeless marriage. No one less than the creator, sustainer, and comforter of the universe is at our service. With His involvement it is possible someday to find ourselves expressing grateful feelings to God, as did the guests at the Cana wedding: "This is such wonderful stuff! Why did you save the best until last for us?"

Afterimage

June 15, 1970

Dear Valerie and Steve,
    Sorry we can't be at your wedding but know the most important Guest of all will be there. . . . May the Lord Jesus bless you on your special day.

                                        Lovingly,
                                        Grace and Harold

3

Where
Is
God?

We had barely been seated and handed our menus when Alan began to pour out the details of his difficult marriage in agonizing emotional heaves, the "can't stop" monologue characteristic of someone experiencing great personal pain. Between interruptions for ordering our food and beverage refills, we learned his wife suffered from terrible premenstrual syndrome as well as bouts of depression. When she wasn't depressed and withdrawn, she was angry and hostile, given to unpredictable behavior and fits of temper.

The children suffered because of her. Alan suffered because of her. His wound was raw and deep from twenty years of married hopelessness. Though we were nearly strangers to him, he was desperate, a man at the end of his resources, grasping for an understanding ear.

For more than an hour we listened intently and empathized completely. After lunch and before the conference sessions were to resume, we found a more private place nearby and together prayed with him—prayers of compassion, prayers for God's healing in his family, prayers for wisdom and strength for Alan and the kids. Valerie penciled the names "Alan and Diane" in her monthly planning calendar. And for the next year, with the passing of every month she rewrote "Alan and Diane" at the top of the calendar as a reminder to pray for them whenever her eyes happened to see their names in the margin.

"Oh God, heal Diane's PMS," she would pray. "Heal their family. Bring wholeness to this Christian home." It was a prayer based in a certain amount of ignorance. A prayer prescription telling God how we would like to see Him work.

A year passed. Once again we attended the same conference and shared a meal with Alan. Like before, he skipped the usual light social banter and plunged immediately into serious conversation. But his story had changed.

Was this the same man? each of us wondered privately. Now we were hearing a different version about his marriage. It was not so one-sided or cut and dried as just twelve months earlier; that is, "Diane is the cause of all our problems, and the children and I are her undeserving victims." We asked specifically about how his wife was doing and waited for the PMS war stories. But surprisingly, he didn't complain about her. Instead, he was excited to tell us about some of the changes in *his* life.

"I now can see myself as a man with some 'hidden' sins—addictions, really," Alan explained. "I've finally begun to realize that I'm a bona fide workaholic. I've been married for over twenty years, but I've chosen not to build my relationship with Diane through the years. No wonder she's frustrated and sad!"

Alan explained that he had experienced a year of clarity, a year of seeing himself from God's perspective. As a result, no longer did he blame the problems in his marriage primarily on Diane and her particular issues. During the previous year he had encountered a kind of personal awakening, a new spiritual vitality internally—to the point that he was regularly praying on his own and spending time with God alone.

"Never before had I been consistent in initiating toward God, nor slowed down enough to hear from Him," Alan continued. "And now our marriage is improving. I wouldn't have believed it was possible.

"Diane still struggles with PMS, but she is less hostile since I've turned around and decided to 'be there' for her. It's interesting; during this year I'd fall back into my old routines, giving in to the fast-paced daily pressures that lead me toward workaholism, which would squeeze out my focus on God. But when I did that, I noticed that the dynamics in our marriage would revert to some of the same old patterns as well. But I'm excited to know that an active personal spiritual life can make an enormous difference in my marriage and my family."

ADDING THE SPIRITUAL DIMENSION

Apparently God was bringing healing to Alan's marriage, not so much by simply eliminating Diane's PMS or removing her struggles with depression, but by beginning to heal him.

A Changed Perspective

Alan had taken some important steps toward God, which set in motion a spiritual process for removing the greatest barrier to the beginning of Diane's healing and the greatest obstacle to their marriage. Alan's perspective had shifted radically. He now saw *himself* as the main contributor to their marriage problems. God is so creative! Alan's changed perspective had carved out enough safe space in the marriage so that Diane could begin to heal as well. During our luncheon meeting that day he was upbeat, his attitude was optimistic, and he was full of awe that God had actually showed up in his marriage in a way none of us could have predicted.

What was happening here? Although everything was essentially the same, everything had changed.

Through Alan's renewed sensitivity to the Lord, a fresh spiritual dimension had entered the relationship, and in one year the marriage perspective had been positively altered. Of course we don't have all the facts of this particular situation—perhaps Alan's spiritual initiative was a direct answer to Diane's years of prayers. Regardless, there were positive signs on the horizon that their long-standing marriage was finally on its way to becoming as good as it could be. Another "successful marriage" in the making, complete with PMS and workaholism! Likely, this couple could still benefit from counseling; but we conjecture that their primary disorder was not psychological, or emotional, or even marital. The dominant problem had been spiritual. Alan and Diane's marriage is experiencing spiritual rebirth.

A Similar Pattern of Healing

Alan and Diane's tension and their resolution fit a familiar pattern we've seen many times in other marriages: healed marriages through a new spiritual perspective.

Within the same month and without the awareness of the other, both Eric and Linda expressed their mutual disappointment with each other to Valerie and me separately. Hearing Eric honestly express his growing frustration with Linda discouraged, even hurt me, because, frankly, she is a remarkably gifted woman. And when Linda dumped her whole load about Eric onto Valerie, Valerie came away from the conversation utterly confused. For years Valerie had commented to me along the way just how much she admired Eric's gentle spirit, love of learning, and even-temperedness.

It grieved us deeply when we came to realize how they really felt about each other. These two are bright, talented, and sensitive individuals, yet they did not see each other that way. We liked them both— very much! Why couldn't they appreciate each other?

Evidently, what Eric and Linda perceived as "bad" about each other had long ago overshadowed what was good. *How sad!* we thought between ourselves. *They each have such terrific personal traits, but the small differences or "rubs" in their relationship are causing them to feel dissatisfied about the whole of their marriage!* They went to counselors and learned the language of *dysfunctionality* and *codependency*. But instead of becoming closer with a greater understanding and intimacy, they simply became more articulate at expressing their differences—almost as if their weapons had become more educated and piercing. They also remained convinced that theirs was an unusually difficult and unsolvable marriage. They stayed unhappily married.

Then financial problems threatened to sink their already overly stressed home. They came to talk. We prayed with them. Time passed and the crisis passed. In the ensuing months we began to detect a decidedly mellowed attitude between them. We said nothing. They still had some apparently irresolvable issues, but their mutual disappointment was much less evident, if expressed at all. We began to put the pieces together when many months later the four of us met.

"Some time ago when we were in crisis and came to your house to talk . . ." Linda began and then paused, recalling the moment. "Well," she resumed, "after we prayed together, a few weeks later we decided to try something for the first time in our thirty-year marriage. For nine months now we have been praying together every day! Eric and I concluded, since praying always seems to help when we are in crisis, why not try it as part of our everyday relationship? The odd thing is, before now, we had never been able to stay at it consistently. If we had only known how much it would have helped us connect. It's like we've discovered a whole new level of intimacy in our marriage."

Like Alan and Diane and other couples, a spiritual rebirth occurred. In the same amazing pattern, everything was essentially the same, yet everything had changed. No longer were Eric and Linda just "staying together." Instead of relying primarily on friends and counselors to help them hang in there with each other, they ventured out, took a bit of a risk, and discovered some spiritual resources on their own. Through a practice as basic as praying together, consistently, they were inviting God into their relationship, and now their lives were operating on a much healthier plane.

What a difference when we view our spouse and lives together through the eyes of God! Eric and Linda's marriage is experiencing spiritual rebirth.

We don't want to be misleading. Of course, all marriages have their tensions and conflicts. Even good marriages—operating with a positive spiritual dimension and fully engaging both spouses—will not be problem-free. But there is a definite before and after perspective in relationships where God has been invited to be an active participant.

A CALL FOR A REBIRTH IN OUR MARRIAGES

Unless there's a proactive sensitivity to the spiritual dimension, even a so-called "Christian" marriage will be characterized by several without-God, after-the-Fall, telltale signs of the need for a marriage rebirth. Any one symptom, if allowed to fester or continue unchecked, could be enough to do serious harm to a marital relationship. The good news: Hope and healing are possible! Though it's not our intent to highlight every conceivable indicator that might reveal potential problems, in the chapters that follow we will address seven of the more common symptoms that appear in most marriages. Also, we'll suggest seven specific spiritual intimacy exercises that will help Christian couples address each symptom and access God's perspective into their marriage. We believe the exercises are powerful enough to position most couples for marriage rebirth.

Again, no couple is immune from marriage problems. Even effective spiritual leaders may struggle integrating all that they know (or even that which they can teach!) into their own marriage relationship. For example, the well-known eighteenth century revivalist, John Wesley, a man of seemingly great spiritual stamina—who over his fifty-three-year ministry sometimes preached four or five times a day, and who rose at four each morning for his devotional time—had serious relational problems with his wife. We're told his home was a shambles. After four years with his wife, Molly, he wrote to his brother Charles, "Love is rot." John Wesley was a remarkable Christian leader whom God used in significant ways to spread the Methodist movement across America as well as to Holland, Ireland, and Scotland. Yet his marriage was a miserable failure.[1] No one, it seems, is automatically exempt from marriage dissatisfaction or outright collapse.

Such marriage woes can happen to each of us, whether we are regular church attenders, faithful members of a small group Bible study, or even pastors of large churches. Ignoring that which can build healthy spiritual intimacy with your spouse, refusing to address those nagging issues between the two of you, or just the willingness to settle for status quo—any or all of these realities could mean you've already resigned yourself to live in a marriage that will never be "as good as it could be."

SYMPTOMS OF A NEED FOR SPIRITUAL REBIRTH

How healthy is your marriage spiritually? Do you know? Is spiritual intimacy something that can be measured on a wholeness or wellness scale? While we cannot be totally definitive, it's our belief that the following symptoms are indicative that a marriage is in need of some degree of healing. Having any of these symptoms indicates a marriage relationship in need of spiritual rebirth.

Symptom 1: A Deep Unmet Longing for Intimacy

Longing to be connected to someone else—to have intimacy—is an appropriate need. But when this craving for intimacy and closeness is not recognized as primarily a spiritual longing—one that God alone can fully meet—there will often be an intense focus on one's spouse to meet those needs, resulting in further frustration and disappointment.

Consequently, the relationship becomes burdened down with impossible expectations. Hostility and resentment build; one feels that the spouse is "holding back." In a spiritually healthy couple's relationship, that deep unmet yearning will be recognized as a hunger that only God can satisfy.

Symptom 2: A "But What's in It for Me?" Mind-set

Whenever married people focus primarily on their own needs, they can become "life-suckers," draining each other. Demanding or imposing perfectionistic expectations on a spouse can rob a home of its place as a refuge, of being an emotionally and spiritually safe place. Creating home and healthy relationship comes from within our beings

—it's a spiritual work. The overall tone in a marriage is much more important than where you live, how rooms are decorated, or any other lifestyle choice we pursue hoping to make home a comfortable place. Home is an attitude that nurtures the seed of life in our spouse whom God has given and entrusted to our care.

Symptom 3: A Tendency to Count—and Bemoan—the Cost

I could have done so much better! the thought comes. *Why didn't I marry someone with the capacity to give me financial security? I should have married someone who could track with me intellectually! Our sexual relationship is so "not there." Our outlook on life couldn't be more different!* These are the bleak thoughts of someone who is assessing the personal cost of his or her marriage commitment. Underneath such thoughts usually are deep pain and regret. Nothing comes at a greater personal price than a mediocre marriage.

We do not want to appear to minimize such pain, which can seem unbearable at times. But here is the telling truth: The focus for a husband or wife without a developed spiritual dimension is always on the pain of self. There is very little awareness of the price marriage is costing the other partner. Marriage problems are misinterpreted when there's an oversimplistic or overstated diagnosis: *She* is the problem . . . *He* is the cause of 100 percent of the pain.

Symptom 4: An Attitude of Entitlement

"I know he's not happy in his job, but so what? His end of the bargain is to support us! Is that asking too much?" Or, "Why shouldn't she arrange her life to accommodate mine? I'm the one with all the pressure!" Marriages lacking the dimension of mutuality tend to be one-sided relationships, almost ensuring that everyday sacrifices are taken for granted. When a couple's "spiritual life" is compartmentalized and segregated from the everyday, living becomes routine with little or no sacred interpretation. The partner who does laundry, housecleaning, or meal preparation is rarely thanked. Work around the home is not seen as ministry to the family, but rather as the obligation and duty that one is entitled to have and the mate is expected to perform. Such tasks are not appreciated as sacrificial service; they become the focus of complaining when they are not "up to snuff."

This is definitely a leaving-God-out-of-the-mix attitude.

Symptom 5: A General Dullness Toward God

You attend church, but truthfully, sitting in the pews on Sundays seems like the compulsories for Christian adults. Prayer is boring. Scripture reading is going nowhere and is mostly avoided. Having a "spiritual life" makes sense to you cognitively, but on a practical level you have difficulty actually experiencing God's presence in a meaningful way—especially as a couple.

When overall spiritual dullness permeates a marriage, then it's time to try other approaches to accessing God. The goal is a new-found enjoyment, connectedness, and appreciation of God and our spouse. When a marriage is coming alive to God, the couple has a re-newed delight in knowing God and enjoying Him together.

Symptom 6: A Sex Life Lacking the Spiritual Dimension

Many Christian couples miss the spiritual dimension of their sexual relationship. Most marriages have been tremendously influenced by the views of our culture. Indeed, the erotic side of romance is exciting and delightful. Frankly, passionate lovemaking is terrific fun! But for the most part this good gift of God has been twisted by our culture, with a major focus on self-gratification or performance.

Spiritually enlightened couples enjoy a tremendous advantage sexually, as their level of trust grows through years of mental, emotional, and physical faithfulness. Christian couples learn to view their sexual lives as an exclusive ministry that connects and magnifies them to each other; they experience the pure delight of mutual abandonment to-gether—giving not just body, but their soul to each other. All of this yields a sexuality that far exceeds the world's version. The couple who begins to connect on an intimate spiritual basis will notice, in very short order, that their sex lives are also improving.

Symptom 7: An Avoidance of Spiritual Disciplines

In a marriage needing rebirth, the spiritual learning curve is flat. Apart from perhaps mealtime prayers or going to church (and maybe discussing the sermon or music afterward), experiences related to spiri-tual life are rarely discussed or shared together. There is little effort to grow the heart and strengthen one's personal relationship with Christ. It's not uncommon for couples in troubled Christian marriages to be lax or completely undeveloped in practicing the classic spiritual disciplines related to prayer, Scripture reading, and personal worship. This symptom may range from mild—those couples who are not resistant to the spiritual disciplines but have no systems in place, to severe—those marriages in which both or one spouse is avoidant or even oppositional.

For couples in such a spiritual state, God never "jumps off the pages of Scripture" to personally communicate to them, because they spend little or no time in Scripture! Prayer does not minister to them, because it seems pointless, like an exercise in futility. They simply do not pray.

"SOUNDS GOOD, BUT . . . "

Jack was a young married man who confided in us about the weak condition of his marriage. He described the symptoms of the marriage problems, all indicating the relationship was in need of rebirth. When we told him that he needed to let God into the relationship and bring His spiritual resources into their problem solving, he agreed; but he also expressed hesitancy with the solution.

"Sounds good," Jack responded after we explained the need for rebirth in marriage. "I can understand on a cognitive level that spiritual intimacy with God would be good for our marriage. But I have a big problem with what you are telling me. How do I access God into our lives?"

Jack then listed his efforts and frustrations in finding the cure. "I have tried the traditional approaches. I read the Bible and don't get too much out of it. I'm not good at coming up with the words for prayer, especially in front of someone else, most of all my wife! To me God is like this vast, lush, harvestable field. I'm thrown into the field and told to harvest, but I don't have a tool, a sickle, or anything. I'm hungry but I'm not able to eat."

Trying to Kindle a Spiritual Interest

Most of us can relate. It's difficult at times to know how to bring a spiritual interest and pattern into our marriages.

Peter comes home from a rousing men's meeting that challenged him to take charge of his home spiritually. Initially he follows enthusiastically the suggestions given by leading his family in prayer and Scripture reading. But after a few days, it just doesn't seem to be working. His family is so disinterested or, he suspects, passively resistant to his spiritual leadership, that he begins to lose heart and finally gives up in frustration. He settles for being a good guy. His family is actually relieved when he gives up his awkward attempts at spiritual headship, and life returns to normal.

During a typical women's conference where Valerie has spoken, it's very common for someone to talk with her later about this same sad story. A heartbroken woman says that her husband is not acting as the spiritual leader in their home. There are many variations on this theme. Some women tell Valerie the husband is hooked on pornography or having an affair; others report that he skips church sometimes for golf or refuses to tithe; or perhaps he doesn't initiate spiritual conversation. Many of these complaints are legitimate; others, though, may reflect a tendency to be overcritical of their husbands in the spiritual leadership department. Almost any imperfection qualifies as ammunition for this marriage war!

Still, regardless of the rightness or wrongness of the wife's basis for judgment, regardless that some of these woman are blind to their own need to feel spiritually superior to their husbands, the relationship is at an impasse. What can she do?

All of these people express in their own ways the cry of the human heart. *When is God going to show up in my life? When will He heal us? Why doesn't He do something? Where is God in this marriage?*

The next day is like the last—always waiting for God to do something.

Where Is God?

These marriage scenarios remind us of the wrenching play by Samuel Beckett, *Waiting for Godot*. Two miserable men wait for Godot (pronounced *God-o*) to come and help them. Every day grows worse. Their lives are gray; even the lone tree is bare and lifeless. The men are beaten and starving. They constantly argue and bicker with each other. They witness incredible cruelty inflicted by sadistic, powerful men— and do not lift a finger to help.

Apparently powerless to help themselves or others, they engage in a hopeless conversation over and over again:

"Let's go!" says one.

"We can't," answers the other.

"Why not?" the question is repeated throughout the play—always with the same frustrating replay.

"We can't go. We're waiting for Godot."[2]

Godot never comes.

Waiting for Godot was written at the time of the Second World War.

The cry of humankind was understandably, "Where is God?" To many experiencing the horror, grief, and unanswered prayers of that time, it seemed He was a "no show." But with a long look back through many decades, with the victories on the Normandy beaches, the end of the Cold War, the tearing down of the Berlin Wall, and a thousand other signs, we understand what those experiencing the heartbreak of that time could not know. We learn that God did show up, not always in the ways we wanted Him to, or with the timing of human choice, but God was with us all the time.

The young man who cannot harvest God, although he knows he is hungry but is lacking tools to eat, is in a sense "waiting for Godot." He wonders if God has been there in the past or is with him now. He needs to pay attention to the afterimages of his life—those pictures from his past that illuminate the present. With a long look back, he will understand that God has been with him all through his life.

Similarly, the father who responds to a call to take the lead in establishing a greater sense of God's presence in his home but feels unsuccessful in his attempts to integrate a meaningful spiritual dimension into his family life is also, in his own way, "waiting for Godot." Look back, sir. God has been with you all along!

The disappointed wife who desperately wants her husband to be the spiritual leader is "waiting for Godot" as well. She, too, needs to pay attention to the afterimages—certain past events—of their relationship. With a long look back, she may see more reason to be encouraged with her husband than she feels at the moment.

WAITING FOR GOD TO SHOW UP?

Is God a "no show" in your marriage?

Perhaps the best gift we could give any couple in a marriage where one or both partners are waiting for God to show up is the one we received from a long look back at our own relationship. Through the pain, through the times of anger and frustration, through the periods when we felt it was all a mistake—what we now know is that God was already there, even back then. Otherwise, our marriage would have collapsed long ago.

But God was always with us!

We did not meet by chance. Nor were our unmet childhood longings unknown to God. He knew us in our mothers' wombs. Perhaps He pronounced our names together, "Steve and Valerie," even before we were born.

God Was Watching at a Wedding

God was there. From the very beginning.

On our wedding day the guests attended the marriage of an inauspicious young couple—barely in our twenties and looking unimpressively like fourteen-year-olds. Our wedding was of little consequence to most of them—just another budget-restrained attempt at elegance at the First Baptist Church. The bridesmaids sewed their own dresses, with varying degrees of success. The mother-of-the-bride's friends provided the food for the reception, and because of money restrictions we had to forego the professional photographer. Out of respect mostly for our parents, our wedding guests carved a few precious hours from their busy lives. Afterward—posthaste and post-rice—they hurried home to try to redeem at least a part of the day for themselves.

But God attended our wedding as well. Looking back, we understand that. Like all newlyweds, we were innocent "newborns" starting life in the confusing world of marriage. That day while our wedding guests talked right through the cutting of our cake, barely noticing us, God Himself tenderly observed our beginning and celebrated the marriage that some of our wedding guests who attended actually missed.

God was there blessing our beginnings as a young married couple, and He pronounced His blessing over our early years of adjustment. He lavished His love on us so that even when we felt lonely with each other, we would never be unloved. He was touched by our joy and omnisciently planned to weave that with enough pain and sorrow and failure to make us mature, improved versions of our younger selves.

We experienced His comfort at each of Valerie's parents' graves while holding our young sons in our arms, their eyes widening to absorb and understand what kind of "owie" could make their own parents cry. God knew that neither of those graves could swallow the future joy even then being held in our arms. In the years to come, the pain of losing parents would be overshadowed by the joy of raising two sons—our lives' most precious relationships.

God was there. Comforting us. Giving us a hope for the future.

God Is There for You

Who waits for whom in your marriage? Could it be that God has already shown up but through the barrier of spiritual learning disabilities you and your spouse have not been able to access Him?

God is with you, in just the same ways He has been with us. Actually, He waits for you to show up!

With a long look back, we recognize the signs of His healing presence in our marriage. We have our own personal marriage markers of His work in our lives that are as significant to us as the Normandy beaches, the Berlin Wall, and the falling of the Iron Curtain is to the free world.

If you will take a long look back through your relationship, you too will recognize the momentous times when you did not stand alone, but God was with you. It may take years to understand what happened. But you, like us, have your own personal marriage markers —spiritually significant places of freedom, healing, and understanding.

Those markers—or "afterimages"—in your marriage indicate that God was and continues to be with you. All the resources of God have been and continue to be available to your relationship. A spiritually rebirthed marriage is waiting for you.

You will need God's help. And where is God? He is here. The rest of this book will help you answer that cry of your own marriage. Here is access. Let us try to help you find Him. As the apostle Paul wrote under the inspiration of the Holy Spirit, "He is not far from each one of us" (Acts 17:27).

Afterimage

February 19, 1980

Hi!-Ho! my Florida dears—My dear dimpled darling, Steve and boys,

Surely have been missing you, especially the Sweet-Patootie Brendan and the little climber upper Justin. Have been hearing about some of his escapades. Must take after his mom—she used to climb everywhere!

Talked to that magnificent husband of yours last evening. He's just really something else. I know you're very proud of him as you are of those two adorable little ones. So glad for you. I know he takes such good care of you. There's such a difference in men!

I understand you are suffering with your sinuses again. I do remember how sick you used to get. So now, my dear, if you run short and need medicine, etc., drop me a line or call me collect and I'll always respond. See? I am enclosing a small check and if you need more let me know and I'll gladly do so. Wish I lived nearby and I could baby-sit for you. Wouldn't I love that?

I just must sign off and get ready for my beauty rest—Ha!

Your ancient old Gram Branham

(A letter from Valerie's eighty-eight-year-old maternal grandmother, Nellie Branham)

4
Longing for Intimacy

Michael's marriage was in real trouble. When he was younger he had been the ideal child, a child whose life predictions pointed to success on every level, not failure. Early on, his parents realized he was gifted intellectually and knew he could be whatever he wanted to be.

There was just one problem. Instead of encouraging him to follow his own dreams, they pushed him into a career of their own choosing. And in midlife, while pursuing a prospering and lucrative career, Michael saw his "success" turn to struggle on almost every level of his existence—personal dissatisfaction, professional disillusionment, and a marriage on the brink of collapse.

"I never wanted to be a doctor," Michael explained to us again for the umpteenth time during the years we had known him. "I wanted to be a teacher. But my parents insisted on medicine." But this time he leaned forward in his sofa and turned the TV on mute. He let the hockey players skate through their game and paid no attention. *Hmmm . . . this must be important,* we thought. *Hockey, his favorite sport, is being put on hold this time.* That day we would hear the rest of the story about Michael, his life, and his marriage.

"My parents insisted on medicine," Michael continued. "Teaching, they thought, would be a waste of my mind. My academic success opened the doors for me to study nuclear medicine and practice in an elite specialty area. I became a critical care doctor. To all appearances I had succeeded. But I can hardly describe the personal cost of this 'success.' My patients typically come to me after they have exhausted all other avenues of medical help. As I try to stop their downward health spiral, my patients and I are literally in a struggle for their lives. That's my world—everyday.

"The intensity of my early professional life was unbelievable. During those early years of doctoring, while I tried to establish my practice, without enough partners to share the crisis load—while we were also in our early parenting years—I began to fall apart. I was crumbling under the stress of nonstop crises. I made no secret of hating my life, hating my work. And I carried a deep resentment toward my parents."

Ellen listened intently as her husband said what she knew all along, but had never heard Michael fully verbalize—his deeply held feelings. And indeed Michael was honest.

"I began to spend the kind of money most people would never have access to. Looking back, it's clear to me that I was trying to anesthetize my increasing anger, pain, and helplessness with bigger, better, and more. Our house was enormous. I laugh about it now, but I even had the stereotypical midlife-crisis vehicle—a really fast, foreign-built, red convertible sports car!

"Additionally, although I was miserable, I was trying to make everyone else happy. My wife. My kids. My parents. My partners. My patients. But I really couldn't juggle all those needs on top of my own. I turned my anger and disappointment with my life toward my wife. The sweet young thing I married had become, in my view, extremely controlling. Ellen's slight weight problem became a major issue with me. She was the symbol of the prison that my life had become."

Michael continued matter-of-factly, recounting a dissolving marriage. "For a year we lived a lie. For the sake of the kids we kept the appearance of normalcy, but we were actually separated. Most evenings I'd come home and have dinner with the family, and then after the kids were in bed, I would go to my own rented apartment. There never was another woman. It was just the closest I could come to running away. I was so strung out with stress I was unnecessarily cruel to

Ellen—I wouldn't even tell her my phone number or where I was living."

As we talked to our friends Michael and Ellen, we confessed to them that for a number of years we suspected they would most likely divorce. Because in reality they were already living as if they were divorced.

"Oh, we of little faith! We thought your marriage was over," Steve said. "How did you two ever get back together? What made the difference?" We both cared, plus we were curious.

"Well, we went into counseling—not together but individually—which helped us to understand that we each had personal problems that were impacting our marriage. That was such a valuable process. Each of us learned that we had issues with our own parents. My issues had led to bitterness and stress. Ellen's issues of childhood sexual abuse—which she had buried away—had led to her sense of needing to be in control. We needed to understand that, yes, we had marriage problems, but also that we had individual problems that required some major work.

"As we began working on our separate issues, there was another dimension to our healing. Something was happening on a different level. It went beyond an intellectual understanding. For a long time, we tried to 'fix' our problems with our own mental and emotional resources along with the insights and suggestions of our counselors. Helpful, but not exactly healing. We were still at a stalemate. Then when it looked like we would not be able to continue trying, that it was utterly hopeless, we both experienced a crisis of coming to the end of ourselves. Even with all of the therapy, the new and needed clarity about our own personal issues, and repeated attempts to reconcile, we had been unsuccessful in putting the marriage back together."

"TO KIND OF FLING YOURSELF AT GOD"

"In frustration and exhausted, we both just stopped trying. At the time it didn't seem like a positive step at all—more like the ultimate act of despair—to kind of fling yourself at God and hope He notices what trouble you're in."

Michael had to leave our conversation at this point to attend to an emergency call he received from the hospital. Valerie and I continued the conversation, hearing Ellen's perspective. "I've never heard him talk freely like this," she began. She seemed genuinely thrilled to hear her husband speak his feelings before her, out loud.

Before we left that night, Michael called back to the house to share the rest of his story. He was very concerned that this part of his story not be left out. Michael had never been so animated as he continued.

"During this time of my greatest despair about life, when I had no personal resources left to cope or fight, something unexpected began happening to me. Phrases from old hymns that I had sung at my grandparents' church began to recycle through my mind:

> *What a Friend we have in Jesus,*
> *All our sins and griefs to bear!*
> *What a privilege to carry*
> *Everything to God in prayer!*
>
> *Are we weak and heavy-laden?*
> *Cumbered with a load of care?*
> *Precious Saviour, still our refuge—*
> *Take it to the Lord in prayer.*[1]
>
> *I hear the Saviour say,*
> *"Thy strength indeed is small,*
> *Child of weakness, watch and pray,*
> *Find in Me thine all in all."*[2]

At first he ignored the hymns' words as "musical intrusions." But then he recognized the personal comfort they brought.

"Over and over I'd think about the words of those songs, and many times I'd cry when the meaning of some phrase made itself personal to me—seemingly for the first time in my life. I believe it was the intense love I always experienced from my grandparents that was the picture God wanted me to remember—the kind of love He had for me. Again and again the healing comfort of God's irresistible love sang its way into my broken heart.

"In what I can only describe as a defining moment of completely letting go emotionally, I gave it all over to God—that weighty unbearable burden that had become my life.

"I began to let God love me.

"Unknown to me, Ellen was experiencing a similar journey. The renewed awareness of God's love released me from the bondage of wanting 'bigger and better' to feel good about my life. A sense of calm replaced the anxiety I had known all my adult life."

Michael and Ellen decided to try again and made adjustments in "some of the stress levels we could control," according to Michael. They bought a much smaller home. Michael stopped trying to "fix" his patients in the areas that God alone could heal. He took on some additional partners in his practice. And, after years of resentment, "I was actually able to forgive my parents; and then I let go of the impossible task of trying to make everyone else happy.

"For the first time in all the years of our marriage I am relaxed. I even take a day off now and then, and actually took a vacation last year. It's like a miracle has taken place in our home!"

GOD, THE ULTIMATE LOVER

How good God is! And how merciful of God to get to Michael before the Bells did! We suspected at least Michael's professional disillusionment might have been resolved by a couple of years of factory work or manual labor. *You need perspective, man!* But God could see so much more than we did. He knew Michael was not spoiled, but depleted. Michael needed more understanding than sympathetic friends could give him, more love than a wife could provide, more than a career change could accomplish, or more than counseling could ever put into perspective. Michael needed to experience—at the place of his most desperate need, at the time when he was most prickly and unlovable—the unfailing love of God.

Like the psalmist, these words became true for Michael: "Turn, O Lord, and deliver me; save me because of your unfailing love" (Psalm 6:4); "May your unfailing love come to me, O Lord, your salvation according to your promise; then I will answer the one who taunts me, for I trust in your word" (Psalm 119:41–42).

Michael's unmet longing went far beyond the reach of lesser loves. He needed God. Nothing else would heal.

Notice that although Michael had a number of serious spiritual issues—bitterness, anger, abandonment of his family—he did not receive God's judgment. Michael instead received God's unconditional, unwavering, healing love. God graciously dealt with Michael's core illness—his isolationism, his sense of self-sufficiency and intellectual elitism, his pride of life, and his independence from God. The symptoms—a fractured marriage, anger, bitterness—could be addressed later.

God's love is always previous—previous to our sin, previous to our selfishness, previous to our mistakes. God deals with each of us by beginning with His love. God will not be content to limit His involvement to a mere "tweaking" of what's malfunctioning in our marriage.

Even though God has a vested interest in healthy marriages—He commands us to live Christianly toward each other—His primary purpose is that we as individuals understand the depths of His love.

THE PRIMARY DISEASE

No matter how far off course a marriage relationship may wander, as basic as lack of communication or sexual struggles or coping with the painful spillovers of living with a workaholic (or an alcoholic)—even if the situation is as awful and serious as involving adultery or physical abuse—God requires that we deal with the primary disease: our sinful choice to be separated from Himself and His love. If our greatest hope is that God might heal our marriage problems by beginning His work in our spouse (who we're often convinced is 100 percent of the problem!), we can't expect God to buy into that. He probably won't. For whether we are victim or abuser in the relationship, the adulterer or the betrayed one, selfishly oriented or the giving spouse, our primary disease is the same. Each of us, individually, must acknowledge our own sinfulness and alienation from God.

God knows what we need. Even more than we need a better marriage, even more than we need a changed spouse, we need to experience God's unconditional love.

David understood this: "Remember, O Lord, your great mercy and love, for they are from of old. Remember not the sins of my youth and my rebellious ways; according to your love remember me, for you are good, O Lord" (Psalm 25:6–7).

THE FIRST STEP TOWARD INTIMACY

Letting God love you is the first step towards building spiritual intimacy in your marriage. Opening up to God is the primary way of accessing Him into your life and your marriage. Receiving this blessing is the first, foundational step toward eventually achieving spiritual intimacy with your spouse.

God's Unique Love

God's love is different than any you have ever experienced. God's love is not human, conditional love. As Bible commentator Leon Morris wrote, it's "a love for the utterly unworthy, a love that proceeds from God who is love. It is a love lavished on others without a thought of whether they are worthy or not. It proceeds from the nature of the lover, rather than from the merit of the beloved."[3]

God is never repulsed by us. Despite character flaws, regardless of what we have ever said or done, God loves us. When no one could possibly love us—when we have blown it with all our human relationships—God *still* loves us. It is His character, not ours, that determines His great unmerited love. Our lives can never be "good enough," our level of spirituality never eager enough, nor our theological tenets ever pure enough to earn His love. Until we understand that He loves us just as we are, we've missed the point of Christianity entirely. Through the Cross, God shows His love and has made forgiveness available.

God has directed all His creative resources, eternal power, and the angels of heaven to get His message through. He will not be stopped by Satan's accusations against us, our own awareness of personal sinful worminess, or the scars left on our souls by another's sin against us. Neither will He let up on our particular life dissatisfaction that bruises and wounds and drives us, humbled, to His love.

Perhaps you struggle to draw close to God as Jack struggled, our young married friend in the previous chapter who was having difficulty "harvesting God," who said he felt like God was this "vast, lush, harvestable field" but he had no tools to harvest Him. If so, it's time to:

Put away the sickles.

Lay the tools down.

Stop working so hard to "fix" your life and your marriage.

Instead, open up yourself. Relax.

And receive God through His love for you.

When we do, we can respond with the psalmist, "How priceless is your unfailing love! Both high and low among men find refuge in the shadow of your wings" (Psalm 36:7). We can praise the God "who has not rejected my prayer or withheld his love from me!" (Psalm 66:20).

"The Blessing" Described

But how does a person "get" this love, or access God into his or her life? How can a person move beyond the theology of understanding about God's love into the reality of experiencing God's love? Author Henri Nouwen writes about receiving God's love in prayer. He calls it "the blessing" of knowing God loves us personally, deeply.

> For me personally, prayer becomes more and more a way to listen to the blessing. I have read and written much about prayer, but when I go

to a quiet place to pray, I realize that, although I have a tendency to say many things to God, the real "work" of prayer is to become silent and listen to the voice that says good things about me. This might sound self-indulgent, but, in practice, it is a hard discipline. I am so afraid of being cursed, of hearing that I am no good or not good enough, that I quickly give into the temptation to start talking and to keep talking in order to control my fears. . . .

The movement of God's Spirit is very gentle, very soft and hidden. But it is also very persistent, strong and deep. It changes our hearts radically. The faithful discipline of prayer reveals to you that you are the blessed one and gives you the power to bless others.[4]

God, the Satisfying Soul Mate

It's unfortunate how many married people fail to receive "the blessing," to experience God's love regularly as more than an intellectual understanding, until they have reached the point of utter exhaustion with their attempts to win love from one another. God's love is more than a particular theological belief. It's a reality available to us. It is to be our daily portion, our eternal blessing, and our life's greatest challenge to fully comprehend. Its reality should extend beyond one's first weeks of conversion.

The poignant silence that follows prayers sounding like, "God, I give up!" or just plain, "Help! My marriage is a big zero!" is fertile ground for God to get through. What looks like a closed door in a marriage can be God's open door. Just when we think we are experiencing a kind of relational dying, God is gently opening our souls to fill us with His living, healing, supernatural love.

But usually, admittedly, God is our last choice. Mostly we would like to have our deep spiritual and emotional needs met by our spouse. We want human soul mates. But even the best spouses will blow it. Even "magnificent" husbands, who generally take wonderful care of their wives, can let them down terribly. We must be careful how we feed our needs. They are unquenchable. Yield to them and they grow to enormous and increasing capacity. A woman and a man need more than another human's love. Only God can provide the love we husbands and wives so desperately (and with eventual great disillusionment) try to wring from each other, by demanding, cajoling, nagging, manipulating, and pleading. God is the only satisfying Soul Mate.

How enslaved we are to this idea of getting all of our emotional needs met by our spouse! But "when anyone expects something out of marriage it was never intended to deliver, he is doomed to feeling disappointed, disillusioned and angry. This can become an excuse for an affair or an opportunity to grow up."[5]

Indeed, disillusionment brought about by unrealistic expectations may seriously damage more marriages than the combined problems of finances, in-laws, communication, and sexual adjustments combined!

A LONGING FOR GOD

The hook of unmet desires can sink deep into the life of a marriage. We remember the Christian wife who, after only three years of marriage, refused outright to have sex with her husband. It was his practice to want sex with her every morning and night—and at lunch whenever he could make it home! "I can't even stand the thought of having sex anymore!" she told us. His unrealistic expectations— apparently the only way he knew how to experience love—had led to deep disillusionment in his wife.

Eventually, the marriage died on the hook of his immaturity— always expecting his wife to make him "feel satisfied." Actually he didn't need more sex. What he really needed was a renewed connectedness of the supernatural, fulfilling love that God alone can provide.

Our unmet longings may be symptoms of a longing for God. In asking our partner to meet our needs, we are settling for limited resources instead of having our deepest needs met by a limitless God. We remember Lorna, who wanted her husband to take up cross-stitching with her. She might as well have wanted him to learn ballet. It was all girl stuff to him. A girlfriend who liked cross-stitching might have met this wife's needs. But, no, she wanted her husband to meet all of her needs. He failed her. Most men would have failed her "meet-my-needs" agenda. Through the years the gulf between them grew, disillusionment took over, and finally the marriage ended in divorce.

Both of these marriages were Christian in concept, but secular in their expectations about how their insatiable needs would be fulfilled. It is a very familiar Christian marriage pattern. Dietrich Bonhoeffer, writing in his prison journals from a Nazi prison camp, noted the same appalling lack of understanding the resources we have available for having our deepest needs filled by God. Speaking of his fellow prisoners, he noted:

> Desires to which we cling closely can easily prevent us from being what we ought to and can be. . . . Almost all the people I find in my pres-

ent surroundings [a Nazi prison] cling to their own desires, and have no interest in others; they no longer listen, and they're incapable of loving their neighbour. We can have abundant life, even though many wishes remain unfulfilled.[6]

Bonhoeffer's description of prison life parallels the description of many marriages. What a pathetic picture he paints—so needy, but hooked on the intent of having someone meet our unmeetable needs. It is a picture of immaturity and bondage—a wife's dream of her husband in a Superman suit, able to meet her every need; or a man's desire for a wife who is the nurturing Mother Teresa type with the body of a Brooke Shields, willing to meet his every urge! Both the needy prisoners and the needy married need a spiritual orientation to experience abundant living, even in the midst of certain and inevitable relational deprivation.

THE PAIN OF FAILED INTIMACY IN MARRIAGE

The pain we husbands and wives can inflict on each other is immense, even traumatic. And sometimes our friends will not—indeed they cannot—know or help. Sometime around February 19, 1980, while my grandmother was writing about knowing that Steve "takes such good care of you . . ." (see the afterimage that begins this chapter), I actually felt such care was missing. The sting from this emotional low point remained for years to come, as I was unwilling to let go of this pain and would continue to interpret our relationship through this incident.

In 1980 Steve and I had been married for ten years. We had two sons—one just a baby, the other a preschooler. We lived in south Florida, far from our Midwestern families. Consequently, there was no built-in backup system for baby-sitting, lending a hand, or sharing the nitty-gritty of our lives. For the most part we were "it" for each other. My father had died the year before, and I still was feeling a period of grief, laden with unspoken and unrealistic and sometimes unmet expectations. Ten years of marriage had strained our capacity to "be there" for each other's needs.

This particular day I was trying to take care of two small children while I suffered from a massive sinus infection. For days my head felt like a bowling ball supported by a straw where my neck should be. My breathing passages were clogged; involuntary self-asphyxiation seemed entirely possible. My throat was sore beyond all normal boundaries—I was tender and raw all the way up behind my eyes. My head split with pain; even blinking my eyelids felt like hammer blows on my cheekbones. My joints ached from the fever. I felt I couldn't go on without some kind of help. That morning I had begged Steve to stay home from work to help with the children, but he felt he could not do that. He had to go to the office. He was needed and expected to be there that day.

Don't be one of those high-maintenance wives, Valerie! I told myself after he left. *Just hang in there. If you can keep the boys safe until Steve comes home, he will take over for you. You can do that!*

I put the baby in bed with me. I turned on the bedroom TV for our towheaded toddler and closed the door, fencing us all in so I could keep an eye on everyone from my bed. The end of the workday found me counting the minutes until my husband would be there to relieve me. All day in bed I anticipated the moment his car would show up in the frame of our bedroom window. Our toddler sat by the window and practiced the ministry of counting. "Don't worry, Mommy. When I count to twenty-seven, Daddy will come home!" That sweet, caring routine was repeated many times until Steve's car finally appeared in the driveway. What a relief! The hours had felt eternal.

He came in the front door and right to our bedroom, but he was obviously on the fly. "How are you?" was passed at me while he rushed to change from his office clothes into his tennis gear.

It was Monday, his sacred tennis day. It had been his established routine for four or five years with three of his good friends—four o'clock every Monday afternoon. He was as faithful to this commitment as he was to church every Sunday—and he was one of the pastors!

"You're not going to play tennis today, are you?" I was incredulous.

"Well, sure!" he answered, not missing a beat. "You know I always play tennis on Mondays. The guys are counting on me. I can't let them down!"

I knew better. I knew he would play tennis that day not out of a responsibility to "the guys." He played tennis because he wanted to play tennis. It was pure, unadulterated selfishness.

I pleaded. I cried. I begged. I told him I had never felt so sick in my life. He was unmoved. He was blind to my tears, deaf to my cries, and committed to his schedule. He did not appear to care in the least.

Just how rotten a husband can a decent man be? I thought. Looking back, it was a small, insensitive sin. But at the time I felt it as much larger than it was.

I completely lost my composure. By the time the other three un-suspecting partners arrived at our house, I had closeted myself and the boys in the shower stall to try to muffle my sobs. Steve bounced out to meet the guys—with a wide smile, I'm sure—showing no indication that anything was wrong. No visible twinge of conscience at the choice he had made. No tweak that indicated he was in the least sorry about our situation.

Gram had said, "There is such a difference in men," but that day I sobbed my wonderment back to God. "How can there be such a differ-ence in one man? Was this the same man who had attended to my needs so carefully in college? Was this the guy who willingly gave up playing his last year of college basketball to marry me, only to end up driving the team bus to out-of-town games in order to put bread on our table? Could this possibly be the same husband who brought me home from birthing our sons to an exquisitely clean house with crisp sheets and a bell to ring by my bedside?" No wonder I was confused. I was living with an oxymoron: a wonderful and rotten husband!

By the time Steve came home that evening, I was quieted but still hurting. I sensed the danger of trusting and depending on anyone as much as I had him. He had not betrayed me with another woman. He hadn't harmed me physically or abused me verbally. That afternoon's neglect wasn't even his usual pattern. But I still felt betrayed. Where was he when I really needed him?

I had heard new, frightening inner voices that day.

"You deserve better than this."

"You need more than Steve can give you." Who was speaking to me? Did I dare listen?

"He has turned away from you when you were most desperate and needy. This will happen again." Swallow the panic. Stifle the anxiety.

MADE TO BE LOVED

Then this declaration: "You were made to be loved."

I recognized that there was truth in every phrase, but where would those thoughts lead me if I listened to them? Was I disloyal to entertain such thoughts? Would I seek comfort in inappropriate ways if I let them lodge too deeply in my soul? I could not let go of a deep inner conviction that I was made for more than tears in a shower stall. I de-served better!

Steve and I believe these voices are insistent calls to our true spiri-tual standing with God. We can hear them when our husbands neglect us for a tennis game (or football telecast). We can hear them when a spouse withholds sex from his or her mate for weeks or months on end. Or when a spouse slams his wife's head against the floor. And certainly the spouse living on emotional crumbs, while his or her mate feasts on an adulterous affair, hears that inner scream. Whatever brings us into such a crisis, we know we are made for better than we get.

"You were made to be loved!" come the urgings against all evidence to the contrary.

Whose voice are we hearing? And how are we to respond?

Steve and I believe the "voice" is God's. God's truth about God's love. A call to our Greatest Lover at the times of our greatest need. Remember, the first step toward having spiritual intimacy in your marriage is to know and accept God's love for you. You were made to be loved—first, foremost, and always by God.

God did not meet me in some special way in that shower stall that day. Wouldn't we all love it if a miracle showed up at the very moments when we think we most need one? But looking back, I recognize that incident as an important and spiritually defining moment in our marriage. In a sense, we had made idols of each other. But we were idols of clay. Although we loved each other deeply, we were imperfect lovers, flawed, given to selfishness that would lead to mutual disappointment and disillusionment with enough time and enough ammunition. We could not provide for each other perfectly.

The shower stall lesson was pivotal for me: Not only must I understand that I was at the end of myself—my resources, my energies, my ability to meet my own needs—but I also had to come to an end of my high expectations for Steve—his resources, his energies, his abilities to meet my needs.

LEANING ON MY LAVISH LOVER

In the bunker of our shower that day, hunkered down against marriage warfare, crying life out down a suburban drain, seeking the safety of tile and grout and things concrete, I would begin the initial redirectioning of my heart towards God—the One who loves perfectly and meets my deepest needs.

It had taken most of my life to "get it." Only heartbreak and disillusionment had broken through my thick spiritual learning disabilities, but I was finally ready to consider God as my only reliable, predictably consistent, always lavish lover.

Spiritual Intimacy Exercise 1
Listening to the Voice That Says, "You Were Made to Be Loved"

For the next two weeks, take ten minutes a day to pray in a different kind of way. Pray wordlessly. Pray receptively. Be aware that it may take a while for your spirit to stop racing, until you stop thinking of words and are calmed enough to first listen and hear God. Let a minute or two pass until you are relaxed and ready to focus on God's love for you.

It may help to pray with your hands lifted up or stretched out in a position of receptivity to God's love; but if that makes you feel self-conscious, just assume a simple position that lets you block out other thoughts. You might also try praying more often during the day for shorter time periods or at those times when you have a real need to experience His love. If you need help to focus, you can begin to pray by meditating on verses, hymns, or spiritual songs that emphasize God's love.

As you pray, listen to God's voice—those inner promptings through His Holy Spirit that encourage or affirm, that tell you God cares.

At the end of the two weeks, tell your spouse about your experience. Share what you learned about God and yourself through this exercise. In particular, what did you learn about God's love for you?

✳   ✳   ✳

Time would teach me a parallel truth. It's embarrassing to admit just how much later, though. Eventually I became aware of the truth about the kind of unsatisfying married lover I can be. We can also give less than we should. Steve was not the only "wonderful and rotten" spouse in our marriage. Selfishness had a female version too.

One Christmas season I unabashedly, unapologetically spent our entire allowance of grocery money on a decorative swag for the fireplace, and the whole family had to live on tuna fish for two weeks—whether they wanted to or not. Later I remembered the many years

when Steve would buy thoughtfully chosen gifts for me on special oc-
casions like Valentine's Day and our anniversary and he'd receive perhaps a card in return. I am also famous in my family for giving the
thirty-second (or less) back rub; forgetting to pick up children (or husband) from barber appointments, meetings, lessons, etc.; failing to fix
daily meals ("Every man for himself tonight!") for two or three days in
a row; or just not getting around to grocery shopping for a couple of
weeks. Many times I've run out of energy before the project I've started
is finished—requiring someone else to pick up my slack. I too could
"play tennis" and turn a blind-to-all-his-needs heart away from Steve.

Just how rotten a wife can a decent woman be?

MARRIAGE BONDAGE TO GOD'S FREEING LOVE

A Field of Satisfying Manna

The selfish capabilities of our heart and of those we love should
sound a great alarm in our soul. But even while we may sense the danger
in clinging to hopes of "soul mating," of life with a spouse who meets all
of our needs perfectly, we continue to stand in the lush harvestable field
that God provides and waste away from spiritual hunger because we
won't eat. God's love has placed a bountiful manna in the field—but
we're looking for the nearest flesh and blood fast-food hamburger joint.

What is that aching longing that you feel? You want a soul mate?
Could it be you long for God and are finally dissatisfied with lesser
loves?

As David Wilkerson wrote, we must abandon a certain marriage
bondage:

> Step out of your bondage of living life only through others. God never
> intended that you find happiness only through your husband [wife] or
> your children. I'm not suggesting you forsake them, only that you for-
> sake your degrading bondage to the idea that your happiness depends
> only on other people. God wants you to discover a life of true happiness
> and contentment based only on what you are as a person and not on the
> moods and whims of people around you.[7]

A Spiritual Intimacy Exercise

We assigned Jack, our spiritually hungry young friend who stood
in the lush, ready-for-harvest field unable to eat, a spiritual exercise.

And we commend it to you as our first of seven spiritual intimacy exercises, each located in the second half of the chapter. The exercises can help you develop spiritual intimacy in your personal life and in your marriage.

We asked Jack to devote ten minutes a day to prayer for two weeks. Importantly, he would pray in a different way daily. One day he would pray without words. Another day he would pray "receptively," listening keenly to God, letting God speak as much as Jack would pray. In all he would listen to God's voice, hearing the promptings of encouragement and care from the Holy Spirit. "Then come back and tell us what you experienced," we told him.

The next time we saw him we asked how it went.

He smiled. "It was really weird. I felt so uncomfortable at first. I couldn't imagine that God would want to say anything good about me. I've been so abused and am such an abuser myself. But I think something is beginning to change in me. Though I can hardly put into words God's love—or describe what God might possibly love about me—I sit and receive. For the first time in my life I think I'm really listening. Something inside me is responding to that idea."

We are so accustomed to the voice of accusation, of tuning in to our failures and shortcomings, or reviewing our inadequacies and defeats. In this condition, we are like putty in Satan's hands, separated from the love and delight of God. To come out of this darkness and into God's light and healing truth, we need to start listening to God's perspective about ourselves.

What does God's positive voice say about you? Who are you? God says:

> You are the light of the world (Matthew 5:14).
> You are a child of God (John 1:12).
> You are a part of the true vine, a channel of Christ's life (John 15:1, 5).
> You are Christ's friend (John 15:15).
> You are reconciled to God and a minister of reconciliation (2 Corinthians 5:18–19).
> You are a saint (1 Corinthians 1:2; Ephesians 1:1; Philippians 1:1).
> You are chosen of God, holy and dearly loved (Colossians 3:12; 1 Thessalonians 1:4).[8]

Let us suggest you practice this same spiritual exercise that Jack did, described in detail on page 70. We believe your will feel greater joy than you have ever known. Experience God's love. In order to fully experience that great lavish love, you will need to come to the end of your self-reliance, sense of life competency, and pride. You will also need to admit your spouse's limitations where your needs are concerned.

THE HEALING HEART OF GOD

Let God love you. Spend some quiet time every day trying to get your mind and soul wrapped around the healing heart of God. Take encouragement in these words from Scripture:

> God is love. When we take up permanent residence in a life of love, we live in God and God lives in us. This way, love has the run of the house, becomes at home and mature in us . . . Well-formed love banishes fear. Since fear is crippling, a fearful life . . . is one not yet fully formed in love. We, though, are going to love—love and be loved. First we were loved, now we love. He loved us first. (1 John 4:16–19 *The Message*)

We need to experience God's unconditional love, because someday we will have to draw upon His supernatural love to minister to a spouse who is unlovable and unworthy. By definition, marriage is a commitment—a commitment to be the one, and maybe the only one, who loves a mate who has become unlovable, who perhaps embraces one who seems now repulsive. We will need to know how to lavish God's love on a partner when our own human love has run dry.

How will you love the crying wife hiding in a shower stall? The angry husband living on his own with his pain and his midlife-crisis red convertible sports car? How will you love the overly controlling wife with a past of sexual abuse or the husband who "can't let down the guys" when your own resources of love are so limited?

We cannot give a love that heals if we ourselves have never been healed. The "glue" of a long successful marriage is not the love we wives and husbands have for each other. Staying power comes from God's love. When we understand experientially what we have received from God—if we are keenly aware of our own unworthiness, unloveliness, and small-heartedness and yet receive God's love—then we can offer that kind of spiritual love to a husband or wife. Such love continues to give to someone, though the person is unworthy, undeserving, and humanly unlovable.

STEPPING AWAY TO COME CLOSER

At some point, we must move beyond human love to the resources of God's love. In what seems like a desperate gesture—a movement away from each other instead of closer to each other, an end of our resources—we join our own souls to God's in a great love relationship. It is the only hope we have for eventually loving our spouse with a deeper understanding and compassion and acceptance. God's love is what turns marriage water into marriage wine. We cannot do that for ourselves.

The first step to a spiritually rebirthed marriage may seem like a distancing move, a step away from your spouse. But by abandoning your expectations of your spouse and stepping closer toward God, you can find the resources to be a better lover in the end. As C. S. Lewis wrote,

> When I have learnt to love God better than my earthly dearest, I shall love my earthly dearest better than I do now. In so far as I learn to love my earthly dearest at the expense of God and instead of God, I shall be moving towards the state in which I shall not love my earthly dearest at all. When first things are put first, second things are not suppressed but increased.[9]

Go alone to that place of healing. Read or quote Scriptures about God's love. Sing hymns or spiritual songs in that lonely place. Allow His love to help you get your hooks of longing out of your spouse's soul. Surrender. Bring what is wounded, what is undeserving, what is angry and unlovable about yourself to the altar of God's care, and let His love consume the burden of dross that is weighing down your marriage relationship. Hear the loving, affirming words He speaks to your spirit. God's love is not just your theological position, it is your daily portion, your source for having your most intimate needs met. Do not miss the greatest love of your life.

We were made to be loved first and foremost by God. "To be loved by God is the highest relationship, the highest achievement, the highest position in life," wrote the authors of *Experiencing God.*[10]

This is the foundational truth, the underpinning so often assumed to be in place when Christian leaders call married couples into devotional life with each other. To share spiritual intimacy comfortably with each other, God's love must be accepted and experienced.

Letting God love you is the first step toward authentic spiritual intimacy in your marriage. When you let God's love replace your secular ideas about soul mating to another human being, then you begin accessing God's love—a love that will eventually bring greater intimacy, greater love, and a greater acceptance in your marriage. You'll have a better marriage than you've experienced until now. *The first step to accessing God into your marriage is to receive and experience His love.* More than anything else—a changed spouse, a better marriage, a deeper human connection—we need God.

Afterimage

Lately I've been noticing my tendency to project my own fear and anxiety onto my family when they are struggling with a problem. Instead of encouraging them I intensify their pain. How can I take myself out of their problems enough to be an encourager instead of a worrier?

For a son starting college and full of anxiety about his major and life direction, what would a life-giver say?

Instead of, "Are you sure you want to major in philosophy? I mean, what are you going to do with it?" a word with life-giving encouragement might be, "You are not lost but in process. God will direct you a step at a time. You have a bright future whatever your major."

For a son unsure of his appeal with the girls, what would a life-giver say?

Instead of, "You know you should pay more attention to my advice. I know how women think," a healing word might sound like, "You know when you are your charming self hardly anyone can say no to you. When I have to deal with your smile, and your funny sense of humor, and your affectionate warmth—well, even your old mother feels like she'd like to swim the deepest ocean and climb the highest mountain to be with you. Believe me, a younger, less experienced woman doesn't stand a chance saying no to that!"

For a husband who works too hard, plays too little, and hardly sits still enough to relax, what would a life-giver say?

Instead of something disaffirming and life-sucking like, "Will you stop that type-A behavior! You're making us all crazy!" a life-giver might say, "Take a deep breath, a big book, and relax your spirit at home tonight. You don't have to do anything, just be."

(Valerie's journal entry, January 25, 1994)

5

Called to Be Saints: Turning Houses into Homes

M ost couples have at least one honeymoon "horror story"; we are no different. It seems funny now, but at the time we wondered if it was some kind of terrible omen, a foreboding flash into the future. Was God trying to tell us something?

Our wedding had been such a happy day, filled with those grand feelings of marriage exhilaration: being pelted by family and friends with rice, laughter, and love. We left the wedding and our single lives behind and headed joyfully into the city and a hotel on Chicago's glamorous Gold Coast to begin our new life. Now we could always be together.

We departed our reception in a 1962 mint green Ford Fairlane, my Grandpa Bell's "prize" before he passed away, and now a wedding gift from my parents. Our guests had really done a number on it. White shoe polish proclaimed in big block letters ONWARD CHRISTIAN SOLDIERS and JUST MARRIED. Rainbow-colored streamers, the bows and ribbons from all our wedding gifts, danced their "just married" choreography behind our car. As we drove it down the expressway to begin our honeymoon, we collected knowing smiles. Valerie looked radiant in a linen and lace coatdress ensemble, complete with orchid corsage. We were obviously, in-broad-daylight, unbelievably happy newlyweds. *Smile with us, world.*

The next morning we left our hotel full of joy. While I loaded the car on that hot June day, Valerie slid across the bench seat to her normal place, far from the passenger window and as close to me as she could sit and still let me drive. As we backed out from our parking slot, I yanked sharply to make the narrow turn. (Grandpa didn't waste any money on luxuries like power steering.) Suddenly my sweaty hand slipped off the steering wheel.

Wham! My right elbow smashed into my new bride's face.

I had landed Valerie a near knockout punch. I could tell her pain was intense. She couldn't talk. She could barely breathe. She leaned her head against the back of the car seat as far away from me as possible. Tears came to her eyes but she refused to cry. She was holding back, trying to protect my feelings. I was mortified as I watched her struggle. The day before she had been the honored bride. And now, this first morning of married life, she was nursing a bloody nose, fearful that she'd return from the honeymoon with black eyes and a swollen face.

I'm sure she wondered whether she should take a more sensible place near the window and whether this new husband could really be trusted to look out for her. Welcome to the honeymoon, Valerie. Welcome to married life!

GETTING CLOSE CAN BE PAINFUL

Thankfully, the black eyes never developed. But our honeymoon "horror story" could be interpreted as a warning about the year to come. In that first year of marriage, we would learn that getting close to someone you love, while wonderful, can also be painful. The upside to intimacy is its closeness and connectedness, but the downside is how it makes us vulnerable as never before. Get close, and there's the possibility for hurt or disappointment. Show care, and recognize that it may not be returned as expected. Or discover through intimacy the parallel truth: that we are all potentially wounding to those we love. It's incredibly easy to deliver near-knockout punches to each other's souls.

Wham! With amazing ease and unintentionality we hurt the one we most love, the one who cared enough to come the closest. We are more potentially dangerous to those we love than we may realize.

Before Valerie and I were married, we never had an angry word between us. *Remarkable!* we thought, especially in light of our nearly three-year dating and courtship period. Of course, we were young and idealistic, but we were also convinced we knew each other very well. *A few minor adjustments . . . maybe,* but both of us expected marriage to be a breeze.

But we had never before lived together.

Early Expectations

As a young man I had built efficient systems into my life that, combined with drive and energy to burn, had allowed me not only to get a lot done, but to get it done well. Once we were married (though I never consciously realized this in advance), I expected Valerie to do everything *my* way—which, of course, was the best and right way. Of the two of us, I was definitely more organized. Surely she would recognize the benefits of my leadership in this area to her life and fall in line right behind me without missing a single step.

The honeymoon was hardly over before it became apparent that Valerie had a mind of her own. If one of my expectations seemed unreasonable to her, without any hesitation she would say so. "Wait a minute, Steve. You mean you want me to wash out the tin cans with soap and water *before* I throw them in the garbage? You can't be serious! Why?"

Well, I had my reasons. "That's how we did it in our family—which is much more organized than yours."

"But Steve, your family lived in the country without garbage service. Here in the suburbs we have garbage service three times a week. The cans don't need to be sanitized—they'll be gone soon."

But I insisted. I just knew that *responsible* adults washed out used cans before trashing them. It was nonnegotiable.

I had developed a precise way to do everything. The laundry, for example. I explained to Valerie in exact detail how I wanted it done. I wanted my pants and jeans zipped up *before* they were washed—don't want that nasty zipper snagging and ruining a sock or a knit shirt along the way. And an open zipper is potentially a broken zipper. Remember, zippers up! Then there were my shirts: It was important to me that all clean shirts were placed in the closet with the top two buttons buttoned. In contrast, a shirt was ready to be laundered *only* when the first and the fourth buttons were buttoned. If just the first and third buttons were fastened and the shirt was on a hanger, it meant I could still wear it once more before laundering. I would not have my shirts, even the dirty ones, being wrinkled in a laundry hamper.

In my opinion, this was a straightforward and very workable approach. However, she found it complicated and confusing. She rarely got it right. Valerie complained that doing my laundry meant she had to "read" my shirts like Braille just to find the soiled ones. "Steve, your clothes get wadded up, wrinkled, and wrung out in the washing machine. Do you really think sitting in a hamper is going to weaken the fibers more than that?"

Another thing: I could not stand clutter. I detested it. I consistently preached, "Put stuff back where it goes as soon as you're done with it. It takes a lot less effort than having to go back later and do it all over again." And I made such pronouncements with religious fervor.

Reason . . . and Then Resistance

Valerie tried to accommodate my demands at first, but as I became more and more vocally passionate about specific details, life became too large of a stretch for this "free-spirited" young woman who was now balancing a full school load, a job, and adjustment to married life. She did not have enough energy or interest to attain my standards of "excellence."

When I could not be reasoned with, she began to resort to her own form of warfare—words. She left no doubt that she considered me quirky and off-center. Some typical Valerie responses: "The clothes piled up on that chair are not complaining, so why are you?" "If you are so concerned about the strain on your pants' zippers during laundering, why don't you start *wearing* your pants with the zippers down? I'm sure that would be less wear and tear on your sacred pants!" "If you were as passionate about Jesus as you are about cleanliness, the whole world would have been evangelized by now!"

Why couldn't she just be a cooperative wife? Why did she have to be so difficult?

When her words failed to change my demands, she went on "strike." She threw cans away unwashed. Her laundry was imperfectly done, while mine stayed unwashed, waiting for the "perfectionist" to do it his own way. "Furthermore," she announced, "if there are other things you continue to be passionately instructive about, you may have them as well. So, in other words, complain about how I clean the bathroom, and I will let you do it. Follow around behind me in the kitchen, cleaning and editing behind a job I have already done, and all the kitchen cleanup will be yours as well. I don't care about this piddly stuff!"

She was tough. *Where did this come from?* I wondered. I was surprised and frustrated; I'd never seen this side of her during our dating years.

It would be fair to say that I was a husband's version of *Hints from Heloise:* a walking, talking, nagging reference manual on how to do housework properly and stay organized. I was a crusading perfectionist and proud of it. Back then, though, I could not understand why my new bride was becoming more and more resistant to my tried and proven methods and more and more distanced from me.

Mounting Tension

There was growing tension between us. For the first time ever in our relationship, angry words were exchanged in those early months.

Later I came to understand that all my "helpful" instructions were like elbow blows—not to her face but to her soul. They had attacked her sense of competency and self-worth. I was being too controlling. So after just a few months of living with me, she had moved her soul to a safer, more distant place. Valerie certainly was not getting the message from me that she was made to be loved—made to be perfected maybe, but *not* made to be loved.

On my part, I was confused. She was increasingly avoiding me and was clearly resistant sexually. Her distance was so painful to me. Additionally, her words jabbed at my sense of self. Wham! She could throw a defensive jab right back at my soul. She let me know that she thought I was at least a bubble or two off, if not completely imbalanced.

THE POWER TO WOUND . . . AND TO HEAL

It wasn't until Valerie's birthday, about five months after the wedding, that I began to realize an important piece of our relational dynamic—that *I* was the one most responsible for creating the tension. I had spent a lot of money on her gift, but when she unwrapped what I had so eagerly purchased for her, she began to cry. I was flabbergasted. I didn't know how to respond; after all, I told myself, *she really needed a new vacuum cleaner.*

Practical? I was to a fault. Sensitive and romantic? I had a lot to learn.

The daily sharing of life brought us into a different relationship than we had previously known. Now we had power—a terrible power over each other's existence and quality of life. We could wound each other like no other people on the face of the earth. We were vulnerable. Like most people, we locked our doors at night and closed our windows to keep out intruders, we avoided places where we might get mugged, we obeyed speed limits—all to be safe. But ironically we became unsafe, almost dangerous to each other's soul.

No one is more potentially harmful than a spouse to whom we have given access to our life.

But happy older couples, and couples in process of becoming happy old couples, know a parallel truth. Intimacy offers another power as well. It is the power to heal one another, the power to bless and minister to one another as no other people on the face of the earth can. Intimacy is always a powerful two-edged sword. It is up to each partner to determine how he or she will use this powerful relational dynamic of intimacy—as a sword to wound or as a means to bless and protect.

PUTTING DOWN INTIMACY SWORDS THAT WOUND

A young and fairly recently married woman came to our home late one night. Sarah was crying. She and her husband had had another terrible argument. "He hates me. He told me so. And I don't think I can stand another day being married to him. He's so self-centered and such a jerk. I'm miserable."

Indeed, they were abusive towards each other and seemingly unable to stop the kind of interaction that wounds. Their intimacy swords were wielding more pain than either of them had known in any other human relationship.

After she finished her "misery litany" and the Kleenex box had become a less necessary accessory, Valerie asked with sympathy, "Sarah, did I ever tell you how terrible Steve's and my first year was together?"

Sarah's Disbelief

Sarah gazed at us from across the coffee table. We could see the disbelief. We knew she thought we were the picture of stability and health. That's one reason she had come to us. She seemed incredulous that we were ever her age and in any kind of marriage trouble similar to hers. Seeing her so miserable so early in her marriage, we remembered ourselves at her age, full of frustration and anger. We felt God's tenderness toward her and her husband and saw them through His eyes. But we also knew that was a perspective they could not see about each other.

"Oh, yes! If it wasn't for our faith in God and our Christian commitment to marriage, we might have eventually just given up on our relationship," Valerie admitted.

"You two? But you weren't as big a mess as Bill and me, were you?"

"In a different way, we were our own big mess," Valerie continued. "When I see you so hopeless like you are tonight, it brings back memories of experiencing some of the very things you're feeling. Listen very carefully to what I want to say to you. Your marriage is not hopeless. You are young, like we were. But you can grow up. And your marriage is worth all the work it will take to mature it. Do you know Steve and I look back and laugh about how crazy our early marriage was? That's how far removed we are from those wounds holding any power over us. When we tell the story about our early marriage, it's as if we are talking about some other struggling couple."

The young woman was quiet now and listening intently. "If you think Bill is hopeless," Valerie continued, "then it is up to you, as the person with the most spiritual perception, to begin to introduce a new level of spiritual intimacy into your relationship.

"Begin to think of Bill as someone to whom you can minister. Or more precisely, think of Bill as someone to whom *only you* can minister. Think that if you don't love him, no one will, and he will go through life unloved."

"He deserves to be unloved," Sarah responded. "He is totally unlovable."

"Really? Does he deserve to die untouched by love? Well, you may feel like he does. But if you want this marriage to work, someone has to walk the higher spiritual road, someone has to live above the urge to win, someone has to breathe life back into a marriage that is dying."

She looked at Valerie and asked, "Are you sure you were as bad as you say? This house doesn't look disorganized. What changed you? Did you just end up doing everything Steve wanted? Is that what you're telling me? Just become Bill's doormat?"

"No, Sarah, actually, it didn't happen like that. You are right about your observations about my house, though. Trust me, when I was your age my organizational skills were a disaster and Steve was a crusading perfectionist. We battled like you and Bill do, but over our own issues. But interestingly, these days if some house inspector visited us, he might find that my office is more organized than Steve's, that I have become an enthusiastic 'nester' with a lot of my energy going into our home and domestic care. We actually are both happy living with order. The difference is the systems serve us instead of us serving the systems. And after everything, knowing what I didn't know when we married each other, I would still have no other man on the face of the earth. Steve is the best."

"How did you get beyond your problems?"

Steve's Changes

"It was Steve. He made the first healthy move. Even though he had been unreasonably demanding in his expectations towards me, he also was the one who put down the damaging intimacy sword first. When I coped with his demands by becoming distant with him, Steve knew we were in serious trouble. He finally realized that his nagging was driving me farther away. If someone had suggested we solve our problems by praying together, it wouldn't have worked, because I was so avoidant of him. The thought of spiritual intimacy was the most repulsive possibility of all.

"But he began to listen to the quiet interior voice of the Holy Spirit. Amazingly, for a young man his age, he didn't wring my neck, but instead he began to serve me. He remembered the Scriptures about a husband loving his wife and took responsibility to show me that he loved me, even if I was distant, even if I never changed. He became obedient to God. He took responsibility for having made our lives miserable, and he also took responsibility to make our lives better. Suddenly, it seemed, he did an about-face and stopped preaching about his systems. Although I would not touch his laundry, he began to do mine for me. My clothes began to show up in my drawers, whiter and brighter and more neatly arranged than I had ever seen them before. It wasn't unusual for the refrigerator to 'automatically' clean itself while I wasn't looking. Tubs and sinks took on a new shine.

"I wouldn't even use the vacuum cleaner he gave me for my birthday. That vacuum had become a symbol to me of my marital unhappiness. So, for about a year, he was the only one who used it. I really tested him.

"During that year, I began to realize how much Steve loved me. I began to remember my initial attraction to his ability to pay attention to the details of my life. I began to reexperience that wonderful sense of being cared for. In time, with a lot of servant's heart towards me, he demonstrated that he was emotionally safe, that my happiness was more important than his systems. I began to be emotionally restored to him. Through the years we've adjusted to each other. He's moved away from a lot of his quirky expectations and standards. He says he's thankful I was tough enough to put my foot down about his neurotic demands, and I say I'm so glad that he showed me how to be more organized. Now we know what we didn't when we were younger: In combination, we are a good team.

"Sarah, your marriage is at the same impasse as ours was. If you could each see each other's soul, it would be all bloodied and beaten by the things you have said and done to each other. Like many married partners, you have shown your spouse that no one dislikes him as much as you do. Every argument has reinforced that message. You have become the most unsafe person he knows. Now you must work to undo that message. Now you must establish the message that no one loves him more than you do. You must help him remember how it feels to be loved and cared for. You must disengage from any response or action that makes home dangerous and unsafe.

"I'm asking you to Christianize your relationship and show your husband God's love operational in your life."

CALLED TO BE SAINTS

Saint? Ugh!

Valerie's advice did not sound appealing to Sarah. Who can blame her? It sounded like a suggestion that she live like a saint, while Bill gets the luxury of living as he wants. Does that sound fair? Who wants to go so far as being a saint in their marriage anyway? We might as well have asked her to become a martyr, or carry a wooden cross on her back, or wear a hair shirt every day. Saint? Ugh!

We admit, there is a certain lack of appeal, especially in the heat of a relational impasse; but unless a couple wants to continue wounding each other with the powerful downside of intimacy, someone must introduce a spiritual dynamic into the relationship. None of us can produce change in a spouse. What we can do is take responsibility for our own contribution to the marriage's pain.

A Positive Spiritual Expectation

We have learned that to make a marriage work effectively, each partner must have realistic and accurate expectations, not for his or her partner, but for oneself. And the most positive expectation is a spiritual expectation: that our life would be a ministry and a blessing to the one who cared enough to come so close. God designed marriage as a gift, a gift that would let husbands and wives experience the most connected and caring human relationships.

But whether a particular marriage is a blessing or an exercise in toleration depends on how we decide to use this gift of God. A successful marriage has almost nothing to do with "luck" and everything to do with being spiritually responsible for each other's well-being. Every couple has had to cross this spiritual bridge with each other in order to move into a happier relationship.

Once a partner has decided to stop depleting life from the relationship, that is also a decision for vitality, energy, and health. Frederick Buechner describes the potential power of healthy spiritual intimacy. Significantly, he likens such intimacy to being a saint, not a martyr.

> And by saint I mean life-giver, someone who is able to bear to others something of the Holy Spirit, whom the creeds describe as the Lord and Giver of Life. Sometimes, by the grace of God, I have it in me to be Christ to other people. And so, of course, have we all—the life-giving, life-saving, and healing power to be saints . . . it is when that power is alive in me and through me that I come closest to being truly home[1]

Obeying God and His Values

Choosing to become a life-giver is a decision to move closer to God's values and away from selfishness and power struggles. God's values for marriage are the most powerful tools available for a successful marriage. The value of receiving God's love was the first spiritual exercise or tool for marriage happiness (see page 70). We will talk about other tools in the chapters that follow, but of all the tools available to Christian couples, the tool of obedience—the agreement to align ourselves to God and His values—is among the most powerful.

Obedience is too often underestimated as a way to welcome God into our lives and into our marriages. But obedience is practically a direct link to God. The often-prescribed devotional life is actually the warm-up for a life of obedience. Obedience is the measure of our love for God. Through obedience we access God into our lives.

Obedience is the race of spiritual endurance, the marathon of the saints. When it comes to marriage, we are all called to obedient saintliness: to give life where death seems possible; "to bear to our spouse something of the Holy Spirit," as Buechner describes it; to create homes of safety where previously only houses stood.

Obedience is powerful. It gives life to a marriage. By honoring God's values, obedience will move us out of our selfish, rational, human, and limited kind of practices with each other. Obedience brings God's love into a marriage and moves it into another relational plane as we honor our spouse. Even if the honor is one-sided or unreturned, life is still being breathed back into the relationship.

Interestingly, obedience is usually the opposite response to our natural human inclinations. The human tendency is to escalate the battle, to wound each other more deeply, to win at all costs. The voice of obedience calls us to serve each other, to minister when our feelings are most raw, to care because God cares.

When we obey, God is honored by our treatment of our spouse and He is comfortable in our home and in our marriage. Our hearts are most at home when God is present. It is God's presence in a house that turns it into a home. In contrast, when two of us are "gathered in His name" yet practice only an agenda of destruction towards each other, then God cannot be anything but dishonored and deeply saddened by our lives.

THE HUSBAND'S KEY ROLE

Showing Honor

Both spouses are to serve each other and honor each other, even "consider [the other] better than your[self]," according to Philippians 2:3. Yet the primary responsibility for showing honor falls directly on the husband. Scripture charges the Christian husband with the responsibility of laying down the wounding intimacy sword first. Furthermore, he should act as the "head" or the "leader" in the marriage, demonstrating to his wife how to use intimacy as a blessing in their lives.

Paul explains this unique husband responsibility in the "profound mystery" passage in Ephesians 5. Paul likens the relationship between husband and wife to the relationship between Christ and His church. Though some men may think or act like it, the text does *not* read, "Husbands, because you're the head of the wife you can assume she'll meet all of your expectations!" No. Rather it says, "Husbands, love your wives, just as Christ loved the church and gave himself up for her to make her holy . . . In this same way, husbands ought to love

Spiritual Intimacy Exercise 2
Becoming a Life-Giver

A practical discipline that has helped a Christian spouse become more saintlike to the partner requires that you ask a basic, but powerful question: How can I make this day better for my husband (or wife)? What can I bring to his life today that will enrich him? For my wife, what can I do or say that will comfort her, lighten the load, or release some pressures?

Ask this question daily; make it a part of your everyday thought process.

Obviously, some days you will be more successful at lightening the load than others. But following though on this simple exercise can become a major turning point in your marriage. It has in ours.

The basic question "How can I make today better for my spouse?" is not just a regular checkpoint to ask yourself. Actually, it's a prayer. Make it part of your prayer life from this day forward. Take the matter directly to God.

✳   ✳   ✳

their wives as their own bodies." Then Paul expands on this idea. "He who loves his wife loves himself. After all, no one ever hated his own body, but he feeds and cares for it, just as Christ does the church" (see Ephesians 5:25–29).

God initiates His spiritual work of turning houses of wounding into homes of blessing by beginning with the husband. Based on the example of Jesus, husbands must put aside that typical "But what's in it for me?" mentality and with Christ's mind-set ask: "What am I *bringing* to this relationship to make it better? In what ways am I giving up my life (as Jesus did for the church) to enrich my mate's life?"

Concerning this aspect of marriage, C. S. Lewis wrote,

The husband is the head of the wife just in so far as he is to her what Christ is to the Church. He is to love her as Christ loved the Church—read on—*and give his life for her* (Eph. 5:25). This headship, then, is most fully embodied not in the husband we should all wish to be but in him whose marriage is most like a crucifixion; whose wife receives most and gives least, is most unworthy of him, is—in her own mere nature—least lovable.[2]

Of course, a marriage relationship is entered in good faith to be a *mutual* giving and receiving. But once we husbands are committed to the bonds of marriage, our primary responsibility is to *give*, not get. Yes, a husband may desire reciprocal benefits, but that's something beyond what we men can make happen. Harping with evangelistic fervor about expectations and all that *you* have coming to you will be nonproductive and disappointing at best. It's a path headed toward marital disaster. The proper goal, or that which you can take personal responsibility for, must always be to give, to serve, to minister to your spouse, to be a life-giver.

Taking a Short Quiz

For the sake of example, let's look at a typical husband opportunity for family interaction. (We know women also work, so please understand that this illustration is not meant to reinforce sexual stereotypes, but simply to illustrate potential problems.) He comes home from a hard day at work and finds the house in total disaster, the place in a shambles. Husband, what do you do when you first walk in? Multiple choice:

A. Kick the dog.
B. Create a scene.
C. Slam down your briefcase.
D. Play fifty questions: "Who left this here? Why is this out of place? Is it any wonder we can never find anything around this house? How did that happen? Who made this mess? What have you been doing all day?, etc."
E. Take a breath, greet your wife and children, and then calmly help straighten the room.

If your answer is A, B, C, or D, you may be a life-sucker in your relationship, someone who is depleting the marriage instead of building the marriage.

If you look beyond the obvious disarray, without negative comments, and with a cheerful attitude "lay down your life" and start pitching in, you are learning to serve. You are a life-giver. Husbands are called to "be Christ" in their homes by such daily service to wife and family.

MAKING A HOUSE A HOME

Displaying God's Love in Our Homes

At times, though, a husband just doesn't "get it." Whether or not a Christian husband ever draws God closer into a marriage through his obedience to God's design, all marriages will benefit if *either* partner honors God in the relationship. Wives are called to serve too. Either partner, having Christian expectations of marriage, can display God's love at home with a spouse.

That is what a saint does, if not for the spouse, then for his or her God. Every day carries the possibility of making life better for our partner. The secret to rebirthed marriages is learning to ask questions like: What can I do to be Christ to my spouse today? How can I be a life-giver?

Taking on this servant attitude over the long haul will create sanctuary in a home and marriage. Essentially, it entails seeing your mate as your primary ministry day after day. It means seeing your spouse through God's eyes: as someone who is precious, someone He has made to be loved and given into your care as the primary human instrument through whom His love is experienced.

Home: A Spiritual Dwelling for the Soul

Making a home, or creating a healthy environment for a marriage to thrive, begins from within the person. It is primarily spiritual in nature. It's building a relationship where life can grow, where there's nurture for that seed of life that's God-given—a safe place where the soul and spirit can flourish. This is the process that makes home a place of sanctuary, where we can replenish and restore our souls. Galatians 5 encourages us to "serve one another in love" (verse 13); in other words, nurture each other proactively. Then the text warns us against ongoing unrealistic expectations and demands on each other, "Watch out or you will be destroyed by each other" (verse 15).

King Solomon reminds us, "Unless the Lord builds the house, its builders labor in vain" (Psalm 127:1). In other words, creating a healthy, flourishing home environment where the relationship between a husband and wife can thrive requires the spiritual dimension.

God has to be in the mix. This same biblical writer, the wisest man who ever lived, gave another marital truth in the book of Proverbs, "Houses and wealth are inherited from parents, but a prudent wife is from the Lord" (19:14). Throughout Scripture God makes it unmistakably clear that He has a vested interest when it comes to marriage. His involvement is absolutely essential for marriages and homes to grow and flourish. And we attest: Left on our own, without God's direct participation in our lives, we would surely have made life miserable for each other.

BECOMING A LIFE-GIVER

A Spiritual Intimacy Exercise

To ensure that spouses are nurturing their marriage to be life-giving requires God's direct help. How can we be consistent life-givers to each other? How can I, as the husband, best serve my wife, my gift from the Lord? How can I, as the wife, create a home of safety for my husband? How can we be the primary human instruments that convey God's love to each other?

We suggest you implement the spiritual intimacy exercise appearing earlier in this chapter, "Becoming a Life-Giver." The exercise will help you answer a key question about your marriage: In what ways is my mate's life better because of me? That's a question every spouse should be able to answer well someday before the Lord, the very One who gave us to each other as husband and wife in the first place.

The basic question, *How can I make today better for my spouse?*, is not just an ongoing checkpoint to ask yourself. Actually, it's a prayer. Make it part of your regular prayer life. Take the matter directly to God.

Words That Soothe and Heal

The variety of ways in which God might prompt us to be a life-giver, serving and ministering to each other on any given day, is essentially unlimited. One of the ways we give hope to our mates is through the words we speak to them—and the tone of voice we use. Scripture tells us, "Reckless words pierce like a sword, but the tongue of the wise brings healing" (Proverbs 12:18). Over the course of our marriage, I don't even want to think about how many times I have been reckless with my words to Valerie. *The Living Bible* translates this same text,

"Some people like to make cutting remarks, but the words of the wise soothe and heal."

"Oh, God, help me this day to speak kind, soothing, affirming, life-giving words to my wife" is a prayer I offer before the Lord regularly. Why is it that so often the people we love the most are the very ones we speak to with the least amount of grace? One of the best ways I've found to help me grow in my ministry to Valerie is to envision her having a personal face-to-face conversation with Jesus Himself. I consider, *What would Jesus say to her today if they could sit down together for a short visit? How might He encourage or affirm her? In what arenas of life might He challenge her? What would be the overall tone of their conversation? What specific input might He share?*

He might say something like: "Valerie, I'm proud of who you are. I appreciate immensely your tender sensitive heart towards Me. Thank you for willingly speaking on My behalf to hurting people. I plan to use you to minister to others more than you realize."

Then, as the opportunity arises, I speak those words of life in my feeble attempt to be "Christ" to her (see 1 John 4:12–13). And I can say with utter confidence, such affirmation does not go unnoticed!

Really Connecting

Another way we can give to our spouse more is to listen more. The half brother of Jesus, James the Apostle, tells husbands and wives and believers in general, "Take note of this: Everyone should be quick to listen, slow to speak and slow to become angry, for man's anger does not bring about the righteous life that God desires" (James 1:19–20). Listening is a skill that requires focused time.

Because I tend to be multitask oriented and aware of all that needs to be accomplished in the precious little time available, this ministry of listening does not come naturally to me. It's a struggle requiring my intentional effort,. Another, almost daily prayer of mine is, "Oh, God, give me Your supernatural ability this day to slow down, calm my spirit, help me to listen up and hear not only from You but from my wife as well." I am increasingly aware that one of the most effective ways I can replenish and refresh Valerie is to initiate conversations where I invite her to talk about her concerns, her pressures, the creative ideas she's thinking about, her dreams, what she's currently reading, and on and on. This is what each spouse—husband and wife—can do for their partner. When we are proactive in this matter of listening—carving out adequate time and opportunity and then asking our spouses to talk—the sense of oneness and connectedness increases.

THE BIBLICAL STANDARD OF HUMILITY

Finally, a word about humility, a basic trait of all who are saints and follow after the "gentle and humble" Savior (Matthew 11:29). The apostle Paul encourages us to "be completely humble and gentle; be patient, bearing with one another in love. Make every effort to keep the unity of the Spirit through the bond of peace" (Ephesians 4:2–3). Never is this humble attitude more important than in marriage. Both husband and wife are to act gently before the other.

Can there be abuse of such humility by your mate? That was Sarah's concern; she didn't want to become Bill's doormat. She is right. There is a certain dishonor in being walked all over. God is not honored when a wife "submits" to angry emotional abuse, or physical pain, or degrading subhuman treatment. Sarah will need to establish honorable boundaries with Bill, including an understanding of the consequences to their relationship and their marriage if the abuse continues. Establishing such boundaries will not necessarily bring her closer to Bill, however. She will need to do more than simply "bear with" or tolerate him. The emotional gap between them will need to be positively filled.

And while God lays this responsibility at the husband's feet, we know that it is often the wife, if she is more spiritually sensitive, who fills this gap best.

A wife's obedience to God is to a call to minister to him. As she looks for ways to speak life and to "bring something of the Holy Spirit" into their home, her heart can begin to soften towards her husband. Perhaps it's because women have motherly instincts that can be used with husbands as well. Who really knows? But women are often the ones in a relationship who "gentle" it.

At the same time, a woman must watch out that she doesn't become a Michal (see introduction) to her own husband: cynical, shrill, and scolding. It seems there is no hardness of heart like the hardness of a woman's heart gone wrong. A wife's intimate knowledge of a man can breed disdain—rushing out to meet him every night with "corrections," complaints, and criticisms, which only distance their hearts from shared life, shared worship, and shared beds.

"Sarah," Valerie coaches, "give Bill your heart. Show him you care. Create a safe environment by speaking healing to his woundedness. . . . See him like God sees him—as a child who needs to be loved."

It is a hard assignment, for any woman—or for any man who shows humility to an unappreciative or verbally abusive spouse. Our hope for Sarah is that she will continue to avail herself of God's amazing resources and superhuman love.

Such humility in marriage can contribute to healing. Indeed, we hope that someday, a young, struggling couple finds their way to the safety of Bill and Sarah's home, where together they will be able to share their own marriage miracle—of how God's goodness helped them turn their house of sorrow into a home of healing.

Afterimage

Today I complained to Brendan about the "rub" I always experience with his father. Steve and I argued in front of him, and I wanted to explain the relational dynamics he had observed.

"I would just like it if once Steve would get excited about the artistic side of life. I feel so lonely when he hardly even looks or grunts at wallpaper books I bring home, or instead of enjoying the color and fabric and texture he responds functionally with something like, 'We aren't ready to even think about wallpaper yet.' I just want him to enjoy it with me. Why does he have to be so functional? Why doesn't he get it?"

I expected sympathy from this child who inherited his mother's loves of art and beauty, things poetic and symbolic with meaning.

But instead of comforting me with sympathy he chooses to challenge me with wisdom. "But, Mom, look at it this way. Because Dad doesn't care about wallpaper and decorating and artsy stuff . . . in the end you get to do what you want."

He's right! Rotten, wise child!

(Valerie's journal entry on November 12, 1990)

6

The Rub: Counting the Cost

*O*ur twenty-eighth wedding anniversary arrived during the writing of this book. With a certain irony we noted that with Steve adjusting to the demands of a new job and both of us struggling to find time to write a book on marriage intimacy, we had actually found ourselves with less time to be together. The opportunity to actually experience intimacy, even while we were writing about it, seemed elusive.

Our plans for an anniversary celebration were hemmed in on all sides. No money to burn. No time for leisure pursuits. Options like an extended trip, a romantic getaway, or a major celebration of any kind did not exist this year. So when the day came—a beautiful blue-skied June Saturday—we simply proclaimed any other outside agenda off limits for at least twenty-four hours. We would just "be" together. A whole rare day alone. How nice. It's what we needed. It would be perfect!

We decided to have one ideal, I-am-so-glad-I-married-you anniversary day. We chose to be tourists-for-a-day in a small historic town. Ambiance oozed from its storefronts and welcomed us inside with promises of treasures artfully displayed, smells of potpourri, and soothing music. A green-shuttered building caught our eyes, and once inside we were transported to another world, another time. The displays were gorgeous: beds lavished in color and swallowed by textured pillows and fringed shams, lights and chandeliers of metal and painted wood beamed the warmth of home throughout the showroom. The hooked wool area rugs begged invitingly for bare-feet ownership; overstuffed couches and chairs waited to womb those who took a seat.

I (Valerie) fell in love with everything. Without realizing it, I was dropping hints all over the place about my newfound passions. Steve had not had time to buy me a gift, nor had I given a thought about something for him. This was perfect. We could purchase a small remembrance, an inexpensive token for each other from this lovely place to celebrate our twenty-eighth anniversary. My words left him unfazed. He undoubtedly felt our budget restraints took precedence over our romantic ideals. Finally, in frustration, I said, "Isn't there anything in this store you like?"

He followed me through the store for a few more silent minutes and then, no doubt hoping to show his involvement, managed, "Wow, that's really amazing how they mounted that fan to the wall. Did you see how they did that?"

His response left me speechless. In frustration, I turned and abandoned him to admire the wall mountings in the store.

At that moment I felt so lonely. At such times it seems we are the original Odd Couple, observing a marriage that is not worth much in the celebration department. I wondered, *Does he do this to me out of a sense of passive resistance to the "be involved" agenda I've set? Or does he really think that banal fan is the most remarkable thing in his sight? It's certainly a safe comment from a financial perspective because it's the only thing we can't purchase and bring home for an anniversary gift, since it's already owned and screwed down. Somewhat ingeniously, however!*

I overreacted completely. But I could not ignore the stabbing loneliness and sense of isolation, the way those words captured the essence of the downside of our marriage to each other, the pain of our opposite approaches to life.

THE RUB DEFINED

The artist and the pragmatist. That's the Bell version of "the rub." Every marriage has a version of the rub: the irresolvable relational friction that can become the focused irritation in a marriage.

Like a Cancer That Devours

Initially the rub may seem like a minor friction in a marriage, but it's a powerful dynamic, with the capacity to grow like a cancer. Eventually, it can devour the other healthy parts of a relationship, until a couple forgets their general compatibility in the overshadowing frustration of the rub. A couple may be 90 percent compatible, but still suffer general marriage dissatisfaction with the 10 percent that's off.

The legalese masks so much: "irreconcilable differences." How can words ever convey the pain of a marriage destroyed by incompatibility? When the rub sets in, marriage no longer seems to be a fit. The easy relating of the early stage of marriage becomes a stage of toleration or worse, intolerance. When a marriage is experiencing the relational friction of the rub, each person is painfully aware of the personal price being paid to stay in the marriage.

In time, every spouse realizes that marriage has come with a hidden price tag, annoyances that if not dealt with can become deep pains which undermine the relationship. For instance, before marriage a couple may have known that their internal clocks were different—one set to early rising, the other to sleeping in—they just didn't realize how much patience it would take to live with such differences in sleep patterns. Maybe one mate prefers active see-as-much-as-possible vacations, but the other restores by slowing down and reading, preferably in the same place every night. And so vacations have deteriorated to arguments about how to spend their time. He adores animals, she thinks they are a bother. Or she feels deprived without pets, he feels burdened with them. One loves theater, the other prefers ball games. So depending on whichever they happen to be attending, the other is bored, bored, bored! She is an extrovert and restores by having lots of people around, he's an introvert, exhausted by this constant flow of people through their lives. He wants lots of children, she prefers quiet and sanity. On and on it goes. There are unlimited possibilities in a marriage for "the rub" to set in.

One writer described the feelings of a wife experiencing the rub:

She really didn't know the problem. For years she'd lived with his noisy eating—soup, for instance. It seemed that he had to make noise when he sipped. But lately it was so irritating she couldn't take it. And why? . . . His laughter at a TV show could turn her inside out. Watching him correct his student's papers. Just knowing he was working at something in his office. Having to hear his strong bass voice in church made her almost nauseated. They'd had a wonderful marriage—28 years. But lately she was capable of taking so very little of him.[1]

Small Things

The rub is small things. His voice. The noise he makes sipping soup. The irritating, intolerable, repulsive feelings that ooze into a marriage and slime away all that is respectable, worthy, and lovely. The heart of stone. The blood of ice. The 100 percent conviction that the other person is unlovable. The heightened awareness of the price paid every day to stay married to a spouse.

Left unaddressed, the rub can become the obsessional focus of a marriage relationship. "Change!" we demand of each other. "Change so I can easily love you again." We wrestle each other's egos to the ground and demand reform, demand readjustment, demand compatibility. Hostility increases when change is slow or does not happen at all. We deserve better!

The "before" of the relationship promises so much more: a soul mate, a twin soul who agrees at every point, whose heart beats as one with yours. Two sets of eyes with the same perspective, minds that know what the other is thinking. But it's not what the "after" delivers: a spouse who challenges, who disagrees, who makes you develop patience or understanding.

THE PROBLEM WITH PERFECT PARTNERS

Look closer at that kind of thinking. What are we really wanting when we go about trying to change our spouse to suit us better? Most likely it's ego gratification—the goal of being married to the matching glove, the perfect bookend, the opposite sex version of our own "nearly perfect" self. We want to be married to another version of ourselves.

How easy.

How boring!

Soul mating is a deep, subconscious river of longing. "If I can find Mr. or Mrs. Right, who is compatible with me at all points, then I will have found the one right, easy, nonfriction mate for me." That thinking runs through all levels of our culture. Just read the classified ads in your local paper of women and men seeking to make a "love connection":

Be My Companion. Outgoing SWF [single white female], 47, 5'4", full-figured, green-eyed blond, enjoys dining, walks, movies, reading, going to the zoo, good conversation. ISO [in search of] SWM [single white male], 55–75, old-fashioned, similar interests.

DWM [divorced white male], 40s, brown-eyed, black-haired, 5'10", 140 lbs., enjoys music, motorcycles, stock car racing, sports. ISO D/SWF 24–42, thin, humorous, similar interests.

These ads might as well read: "SWF, or DWM, ISO myself." For the narcissistic goal is to find an ideal version of oneself.

BEYOND AN EASY SOUL MATE

Here's another description of the spouse we all want: "Someone to whom we feel profoundly connected, as though the communicating and communing that take place between us were not the product of intentional effort, but rather a divine grace. This kind of relationship is so important to the soul that many have said there is nothing more precious in life."[2]

That definition of a soul mate appears in Thomas Moore's best-seller, *Soul Mates: Honoring the Mysteries of Love and Relationship*. According to Moore, we're looking for spiritual connectedness that happens spontaneously as a kind of magical easy relationship, needing little effort or intentionality. That sounds a lot like most relationships in the first early hormonal, serotonin flowing "before" days of easy love. Even if we could find the secret to making that kind of love last, the concept is still flawed because "easy love" is not a strong enough foundation on which to build a long "after" relationship.

Loving Through Thick and Thin

What makes a marriage relationship valuable? Looking at another kind of intimate relationship can help uncover the answer. What makes us love our children through thick and thin? With parents, the deepening attachment to their children develops in the continual daily sacrifices made to meet their needs. The parents lay down their pressing personal priorities and crises for the sake of a childish, impatient need. During the first years they devote hours rocking a crying child to sleep; later they may sit bored, bored, bored at Little League games. They hurt with the child when he has no friend. Parents willingly share nights of homework with a child who is convinced he or she is intellectually dwarfed. A father may pray in the darkness by the bed of a child who is afraid. A mother may give nights of cleaning puke from walls, beds, herself, and the sick, little wide-eyed child.

But are we put off by all of this? No. Our parental sacrifices make our children all the more precious, loved, and valuable. What we invest in we care about. The child we adore in the nursery of the hospital, through years of care and sacrifice, becomes the child we would not hesitate to give our lives to save. Love grows through sacrificial care.

Relational value for children or spouses flows out of the same hard places. That is how a husband and wife can love each other through thick and thin. There is no easy connecting. Married love "sticks" through things like arguments that establish honorable boundaries with each other, through debates over painting and wallpapering preferences. Here is love that gives value to one's spouse:

- Refusing to leave when the pressing self-preserving voice screams "Flee!"
- Learning to laugh at yourself through your spouse's eyes
- Finding meaning in life that's mutually shared
- Accepting the daily mutual sacrifices to make life work
- Holding a crying husband whom life has beaten down, which requires putting aside a wifely insecurity long enough to love what is wounded
- Enduring the times of depression and grief and loss endured together

This is real love.

An easy soul mate may make the heart beat faster for a while; the "perfect" times together may seem like something out of the ordinary and therefore special, but they pass. A soul mate is like a fast roller-coaster ride: three screams, two tight turns, one upside-down loop and the ride is over. The investment of lifetime lovers will provide a return that is much more meaningful and enduring. How? Committed lovers have a quality of life that is profoundly connected; a richness of relationship that will not be repulsed, pushed away, or destroyed without a fight; a knowing and being known that provides the basis for the deepest human intimacy.

Years into the marriage, the relationship just keeps giving a return on the investment—a growing, lasting intimacy.

A Love We Fight For

A hard-won marriage should be cherished. It is potentially rich in diversity and understanding, marked by an amazing, seemingly irrational commitment that sticks together through the hard times. It's watered by tears, tempered by frustrations, and baptized in forgiveness. This loving relationship is the product of a lot of hard relational work.

Such love you must fight for, sacrifice for, work for. Marital happiness cannot be based on instant "magic." It takes years of committed care. What makes a marriage stick? Any of the following investments:

- Devotion to each other's care through hard relational work
- Devotion through compromise and commitment
- Offering to our spouse mercy, clemency, forgiveness, and love when the other is past feeling for
- Continuing to give what has not been earned or deserved

This is the steady movement beyond what is easy and immature. It continues through the years. There is something of the wondrous in a marriage that is experiencing "divine grace"—knowing God Himself is helping to move us beyond our human limitations and methods of dealing with each other. For all who have experienced such a marriage, who realize and acknowledge that God has moved you to another dimension of relating to each other, it is like having a marriage miracle with your names written all over it.

THE SPIRITUALLY CONNECTED COUPLE

The Christian concept of marriage is very different from our cultural expectations for "spontaneous combustion." The Christian concept of marriage is healthier, more realistic, and full of the kind of grace that can lead to the deepest understanding and compatibility. "The two shall become one" of Scripture represents marriage as the coming together of two divergent, separate, unique individuals. It has less to do with spontaneity and much more to do with process, with what happens over time together.

When we look for soul mating in our marriages, it's as if we expect to find two pieces of paper that are identical and, therefore, compatible. But the Christian view of marriage is more like a sheet of parchment: two unmatched layers of hole-filled, unusable, fragile, limp paper fused together making a complete, strong, functional, and actu-

ally quite beautiful whole. The holes, while invisible to the eye, are actually responsible for the wonderful, nubby, individualized texture of
each sheet of parchment.

The blending into one whole, while maintaining individuality, is a
miraculous reality worthy of celebration. The "two shall become one"
of Scripture indicates that a couple's spiritual connectedness covers
their individuality and melds them together. It is not their similarities
that make them compatible or whole, but the "twoness," the differences, the separateness, the unique blending of two personalities together. In other words, it's the *process* of working out the differences in
our marriages that eventually melds us to each other.

A couple may have practically no similar interests and have a wonderful marriage if they are spiritually fused. And the opposite is equally
true. A couple can have many similar interests and still be incompatible because there is no grace, no mercy, no spiritual tenderness, or no
operating love of God in the relationship. Spiritual connectedness, not
ego-connectedness, creates the deepest relationships between men
and women.

RESPONDING TO THE REPULSIVE

But what if your spouse is truly repulsive? We thought of that one
night when Valerie and I enjoyed the pleasure of an evening dining
out. I had picked a small restaurant for its quaintness and excellent
food. I knew she would like the place. Tablecloths, candlelight, and a
cozy fire made for the most intimate ambiance. We splurged. Valerie
ordered a special salmon over pasta; while I requested steak au poivre.
Everything was perfect. It was a major romantic coup . . . until we
heard the man seated behind us.

He had begun to hum along with all the background music. First,
he "left his heart in San Francisco." Then he attempted to "fly me to
the moon." He was "steppin' out with my baby" on "a foggy day." And
"it didn't mean a thing if it ain't got that swing!" On top of all of this he
was "stuck on you." How did he do it? Amazingly, he performed the
practically impossible anatomical feat of simultaneously swallowing
and humming.

Curiously, his wife seemed unaware of his continuing "contribution" to our evening. *How can she stand that?* we wondered. This guy
knew *all* the songs.

In the end, our problem with the ever-present serenade was unex-
pectedly solved. A violin soloist struck up a flaming rendition of *The*

Flight of the Bumblebee. Pavarotti himself could not have performed those roulades. And this guy was no vocal gymnast. Ah . . . mercy. For the first time that evening he was silent. We could hardly stop laughing.

He made *us* crazy! But the major question we were really curious about: "How does his *wife* put up with that?"

"But, that's really not much," a husband protested when we told him about "the hummer" and how we need to be tolerant of each other's irritating sides. "My wife and I aren't just incompatible. We live on completely separate planes."

How lonely. How difficult. What if the differences in a marriage seem irreconcilable—more than an occasional stab of loneliness, more than an occasional irritating habit or embarrassing personality quirk?

How can a refined woman deal with a marriage rub to a husband who is a public boor—an in-your-face, belching embarrassment to her with his constant barrage of banal, break-the-sound-barrier uninformed opinions? How can she be anything but deeply offended by him? What about the husband who is afraid to come home with company for fear they will see the slovenly way his wife keeps herself and her home? Every time he walks through their front door, sees the sink overflowing with days of dirty dishes, picks his way across a floor strewn with debris, gets a glance of her dirty fingernails and ratty hair, he fights the urge to leave her.

What if love has turned to repulsion? What if a wife is an organized, capable human being but her husband proves innately unable to hold a job and support the family? He has worn out the recliner through the years while she struggles to be the sole provider. The very sight of him fills her with resentment and anxiety. And what about the man locked in marriage with a woman-child, a wife who never grew up—the temper tantrums, the selfish drain on his energy and time, the whining and demands, the lack of taking responsibility? Can a husband do more than suffer through the years with her arrested development? What about people whose marriage lot in life is to live with a controller—someone who withers them moment by moment under a barrage of critical assessment, who submits their every move to their own superior editorial standards, someone no one can stand being with because of how competent they are in making others feel so incompetent?

How incredibly hard.

But are marriages like these excused from the biblical mandate to love each other? Is it enough to simply tolerate a difficult spouse?

The truth is, we *all* will be repulsed by our spouses at times, according to marriage counselor Larry Crabb. And we can do much more than simply tolerate our mate.

> No matter how intimate their relationship or firm their commitment, all married people find their mates annoying or maddening at times. So how is one to *accept,* not just endure, an ill-mannered or irritating spouse? . . . The Bible requires that we do more, far more, than tolerate each other. We are instructed to accept each other as God accepts us (Rom. 15:7). We are to forbear one another in love, and this involves something different than putting up with our mates with a resigned sigh. . . . Somehow we are supposed to accept each other.[3]

There are no "permission to withhold love" clauses from God's ideal of love and acceptance in marriage. But how do we move beyond cold toleration or hot confrontation in our lives? As only marriage partners can, through the day in and day out of shared life together, we become programmed to hypersensitivity about each other's repulsive rub: the comment about how a wall fan is mounted (that no one else would react to!), the sound of his slurping of soup, the reality of living intimately with another flawed human being. Without intervention, the repulsive response comes to the slightest stimuli from a spouse. After years of this kind of programming, to change our responses will require a very intentional, disciplined approach to our spiritual formation towards each other.

It will take a powerful spiritual exercise to move couples beyond lifetime tolerators, to lifetime lovers; to move beyond tweaking to an entirely different approach to thinking about how each other's lives affect our spiritual formation.

It will take a spiritual rebirth. The next chapter invites you to participate in a spiritual exercise that can bring such a rebirth.

Afterimage

Today I read that in Victorian England the ladies carried nosegays [small bunches of flowers] as they walked through the sewage-laden, garbage-strewn streets of London. When the street smells became overwhelming, the women would hold the nosegays under their noses to help them continue on their way.

There is a parallel spiritually—a nosegay for the spirit. When life becomes overwhelming, full of disappointment and frustration, when the "going gets tough," when . . . I think I can't continue under some current problem or when I'm tempted to give in to discouragement, I can revive my spirit with the nosegay of gratefulness.

A grateful spirit refocuses my attention and reminds me that, regardless of my personal struggles, nothing can separate me from the love of God. I can feel overwhelmed or I can feel blessed—the choice is mine.

Though the fig tree does not bud
and there are no grapes on the vines,
though the olive crop fails
and the fields produce no food, . . .

Yet I will rejoice in the Lord,
I will be joyful in God my Savior. (Habakkuk 3:17–18)

(Valerie's journal entry on March 11, 1992)

7

Smoothing
the
Rub

"*P*erfect love means to love the one through whom one has become unhappy." That definition of a whole and healthy love, offered by Søren Kierkegaard, seems both a contradiction and impossible to achieve. But that is what perfect love requires and it can be accomplished—but only through the grace of God. Such love means accepting the rub we feel from our partner at various times in our marriage.

How do we handle that friction in our marriage relationship so that we embrace our spouse and grow our marriage? The answer is found in developing spiritual intimacy with God in our personal life and in the relationship with our spouse.

The spiritual intimacy exercise in this chapter is summarized on pages 120–21, but we will discuss it throughout the chapter, for personal and marital spiritual intimacy are the keys to smoothing the husband/wife differences in marriages, as we will see.

Smoothing the rub requires a couple to take three steps: (1) identify the rub; (2) accept the rub; and (3) discover the grace to celebrate each other.

STEP ONE: IDENTIFY THE RUB

Learning About the Truth

The first step in smoothing the rub is to recognize it. Most couples will not struggle with this step. Complaining about or quarreling over the rub is often the place where you are stuck on *replay* in your relationship. The value in identifying and articulating this struggle—in the light, in the open, to each other—is learning the truth. Stating the rub will clarify your struggles. With some relief the marriage can be viewed in the light of this reality. It is a marriage with one main difference, not multiple difficulties. Understanding this truth is good news.

So, for instance, the rub in the Bell marriage is that we are frustratingly different in temperament. The easiest way for us to explain it is to take you to the Hundred Acre Wood, where Winnie the Pooh lives. Steve is like Pooh's friend Tigger—happy, in-your-face, hyperactive Tigger. Steve is passionate for process, practicality, and order—and loads of fun! There is little calm water when he is around. Valerie, on the other hand, is like Pooh's gentle but contemplative friend Eeyore—the-sky-is-falling, given to sadness, poor-me Eeyore. Valerie is passionate for beauty and expression, a frustrated artist with no medium but her home. She adores calm water.

Our rub intensifies! Steve has the "gift" of picayune. He cares about details. He can be an overbearing perfectionist—but with a smile. When Steve creates, he charts his course—figures out where he's going and then begins. In contrast, Valerie sees and cares about the big picture only. Details are a bother. Personal space, relational peace, and beauty are all core values to her. When Valerie creates, her free spirit sets off from shore without a plan, ready to enjoy the trip, trusting that creativity will win out and that eventually her craft will end up somewhere interesting and worthwhile.

Just imagine some of our "conversations" over the years—the pragmatist and the artist!

Remember, by definition, the "rub" is that which is innately different and mostly unchangeable about each other. At a certain point in our marriage, to our considerable dismay we realized that no amount of counseling in the world could "change" these innate differences of ours. Yes, we could talk about them. Yes, we could learn to manage them better. We could even grow to understand and adjust to each other more fully and graciously. But without something as drastic as a lobotomy on the frontal lobe, the seat of our personalities, we would never be able to change these pieces of who we are—no matter how often we wrestle each other's egos to the ground arguing about our frustrations with this rub.

Expecting the Differences

We learned this after years of struggling with our innate differences. These distinctives, these personality traits or preferences, represent how God has uniquely wired each of us. It's not that one way is superior to the other. It's just that we are very, very different. Our nearly opposite perspectives, we've concluded, are genetically ingrained. So we can expect these differences to show themselves in multiple ways all throughout our relationship. Fight it, or take advantage of it. That's the choice.

Recognizing and naming these differences is the beginning step of dealing positively with the marriage "rub." Identify the differences. Find the common theme beneath them. This approach should help define the "rub." For most couples, this part of the exercise will likely not be hard, because most are already aware of the personal costs involved in staying together.

STEP TWO: ACCEPT THE RUB

Changing Perspective, Not One's Spouse

If it is good news to learn that multiple manifestations of marriage difficulties often can be boiled down to a primary root cause, then it is equally bad news to realize that we will not be able to "fix" each other entirely, if at all. To create a healthy relationship we will have to change our perspective instead of trying to change our spouse. This requires practicing the perspective of acceptance. Grown-up, realistic acceptance is the second step in smoothing the rub.

When a couple becomes dissatisfied and focused on the rub, they consciously or subconsciously take on the impossible task of trying to change each other. At this point a couple's marital satisfaction is enormously compromised. Some couples hold amazingly unrealistic expectations about change. They feel they should be able to "fix" everything about their lives. Often couples will seek counseling, hoping for the undeliverable. When the agenda to change each other—or the idea that someone else can fix their marriage—fails, it's not uncommon for a sense of despair, a hardness of heart, or the desire to escape to set in on one or both partners.

Even the best marriage counselor in the world will not be able to "fix" a marriage with unrealistic expectations. However, effective marriage counselors can help with change—in terms of altering perspectives or expectations to bring more understanding, acceptance, and grace into a relationship. In the end, the greatest service a counselor may provide is to help such couples understand that when it comes to innate differences, change is sometimes impossible.

Still Disagreeing, Still Loving

About five years into our marriage, we attended a special fiftieth wedding anniversary celebration. We were honored to be seated at the table with the celebrating couple. We took advantage of the opportunity, asking question after question about their long-term relationship, pumping them for all we could learn—after all, they were survivors! They were most responsive to our eager inquiries.

As they talked about their enduring marriage, we were surprised to learn that they were still struggling with some of the same issues that had troubled their early marriage. They still disagreed about how to handle the kids—and the "kids" were all married and long flown from their nest. They had completely different views about quality of life issues: she was a homebody; he wanted to live out of a suitcase. *After all those years,* we wondered, *how can they still be unresolved about these things?*

We felt sorry for them and thought it was a great misfortune. What a shame that they hadn't "grown" beyond that point!

We were so young and naive and judgmental.

Now we replay their story in our minds with a different interpretation. Now we understand. She was innately a homebody, as committed to family and rooted into security as he was a man with wings on his feet, a doer and goer, willing to be God's man anywhere in the world. Deep into our own anniversaries, we recognize that their marriage tensions could not be realistically "grown" beyond.

Laying Down the Weapons of Change

It is extremely important that couples come to the place in marriage where they lay down their "weapons of change" for each other. When a couple recognizes an unmoveable barrier to their marriage satisfaction, they must decide which relational road to travel. They can become aware that their basic connecting needs are unmet, resist the situation, and move farther into selfish thinking patterns. Or they can listen to the inner voice that consistently reminds them that they were made to be loved. That interior voice insists we face God, our ultimate Lover. When we come to the end of our expectations for human connectedness and understand that God alone is our soul mate—and that only through mutual spiritual formation to His love can we be at peace with each other—then we have taken an enormous stride towards spiritual intimacy in marriage. As Crabb has noted:

> We must grasp the truth that our needs are met in Christ by meditating on our riches in Him, aggressively telling ourselves that we are worthwhile even when we feel most rejected and useless . . . When our minds visualize what our spouses did to us [or what they cost us] we must forcefully remind ourselves that whatever has happened does not alter the fact that I am secure in Christ's love and significant in His plan. The key is to never allow the memory of an offending event to run through our minds without immediate restating to ourselves the truth of "needs met in Christ."[1]

Consider that God's plan for meeting our needs ultimately must mean a restoring of our brokenheartedness to His love. We were made to be loved, made for deep connection and complete acceptance. Our deepest needs are met only by God. He loves us too much to allow us lasting satisfaction with lesser loves.

The despised marriage rub is in actuality a sign of the grace of God, increasing our sense of aloneness in this world, but also redirecting us towards the greatest love we've ever known—and to our only hope for making our marriages whole or the best they can be.

The marriage rub often functions to bring each other into balance, under the umbrella of God's heart, not by becoming the same, but rather through completing the holes in each other's lives.

STEP THREE:
DISCOVER GRACE TO CELEBRATE EACH OTHER

But does a couple have to stay locked into frustrated toleration with each other? No. We can change our perspective on the rub. The third step to dealing with the rub moves beyond identification and acceptance. It is learning to focus not on the cost to oneself, but on the cost to our mate in giving his or her life to us in marriage.

How is it possible to bring this kind of grace-filled love into a marriage that genuinely accepts and celebrates each other's differences? Let us suggest a two-part "reprogramming" exercise that we've found extremely helpful in moving both of us toward this discovery of needed grace that has enabled us to embrace—and yes, even celebrate—our differences. First, consider the whole cost of marriage. Second, express gratitude for the differences in the marriage.

Part 1. Counting the Whole Cost of the Marriage

Every time a disparaging, coldhearted thought about the relationship emerges, stop in your tracks! Then, literally reverse the thought process. Instead of where you were going, think of that which it has cost your partner to be married to *you;* come up with at least five things. Are you realistic and humble enough to understand that living with you may also be difficult? Never forget: The rub typically goes both ways.

Once you've thought this through, take the next step and write down these five things. Then to complete this part of the exercise, you need to go ahead and share your insights with your spouse. Humble yourself and learn to give to your spouse the grace you have received from God.

What does this really look like in a marriage? Let us illustrate from our own lives. When Steve made the comment about how uniquely a fan was connected to a wall, Valerie's first reaction was to quickly count the cost of her marriage as she saw it. Following through with what we're suggesting here, however, requires Valerie learning to make a complete shift in her mind, from focusing on her disappointment with Steve to highlighting what it cost *Steve* to be married to *her.*

Both of us have written such lists. Whenever we're tempted to count what our marriage is costing us personally, we now are much more apt to rehearse the following thoughts in our heads instead of playing the old tapes that focused on our dissatisfaction with the other.

Here's a look at Valerie's list:

WHAT I KNOW THIS MARRIAGE COSTS STEVE

1. Because Steve is so good with details and I am so weak, he deals with most of the functional, responsible areas of life—paying bills, car and house maintenance, filing income taxes, keeping the family calendar, filling out forms of all kinds, and more.

This leaves me with the more expressive, creative areas—putting our home together, cooking, decorating, gardening, and having the time to focus on my writing and speaking ministries. We function well this way, but I definitely think I have the better end of the deal. At this point, I don't even back him up in his areas. This is an enormous time commitment on his part just to stay on top of all of our lives.

2. Steve funds my artistic expressions. And my "dreams" are not always cheap. While I also work—as a freelance writer and speaker for conferences and church groups—Steve brings in the bulk of the family income. With the discretionary dollars we have, I'm sure he might enjoy spending it in other more masculine ways—tools, sports pursuits, motorcycles. However, I have boundless enthusiasm for wallpaper, gardening "extras," old furniture finds, art, etcetera, and Steve consistently sacrifices "his stuff" to accommodate my interests on limited funds.

3. My speaking and traveling also costs Steve. Over the past decade, whenever I've been away he's filled in as "Mr. Mom." For much of the year—especially in the fall and spring—we don't have normal weekends, normal social lives, normal anything because of what I feel called to do. This costs Steve personally, yet he continues to encourage me to develop fully my spiritual gifts and to invest myself in that which impacts the kingdom. Many of the details which support me in this kind of ministry—the packing and shipping of books, the tracking of inventories and accounting issues—all of this comes out of his "free" time and energy.

4. Steve is the original male bonder. He enjoys being one of the guys. But through the years he has tempered his love of sports with balancing the needs of his family. I feel badly when I realize how rarely he plays anymore. The boys and I are a priority to him, and his other loves take a backseat most of the time.

5. It costs Steve a certain level of his kind of fun to be married to me. His active "going" and "doing" tendency is tempered by me. I often rain on his fun parade by narrowing his capacity for many relationships to just a few comfortable friends, slowing his pace to quiet evenings at home. And over the years he's honored my wishes whenever I've "vetoed" his desires for certain adrenaline rushes like bungee jumping, skydiving, and anything having to do with the pursuit of speed.

Steve has created a similar list called "What I Know This Marriage Costs Valerie" Here are his five items:

1. Typically I'm not quick to jump at Valerie's next great creative idea or project for the house, the garden beds, antique piece of furniture found in somebody's junk pile, or whatever. Instead, I readily plunge ahead to what it is going to cost to make it happen in terms of money and especially *my* time. Rather than entering enthusiastically with Valerie and her sheer joy in just "dreaming" about whatever it happens to be (fully realizing that it won't necessarily require much time or money at least today), my tendency is to drag my feet "skid marking" the process. Whenever she has to "pull me along," I know it's like sucking life from her. My quickness to hide behind "I'm just being realistic and practical" quenches her spirit.

2. Because of my commitment to "excellence" (OK . . . so I have perfectionistic tendencies!), whenever working on a project that Valerie has "sold me" on, I typically slow down progress way beyond the time frame she anticipated. After all, I only want to do this once, so if it's going to be done it will be done right the first time. I know this requires a lot of extra patience on Valerie's part because she honors my pace, though left to her it would have been accomplished in half the time.

3. Because I'm the one with a full-time job, my agenda almost always prevails. Even our boys' needs take priority over her own. Plus, because her schedule is usually the most flexible, she's the one who ends up putting out any "family fires" and picking up the slack or scattered pieces of all of our lives.

4. Valerie is an artist at heart. She's driven to create an atmosphere of love, beauty, and calm all around her. When I allow myself to become so busy and harried with the responsibilities and pace of life and don't even notice her latest creation—something she's spent hours on—or at most I pass along a flippant "That's nice . . . ," I know it makes her feel unappreciated, maybe even lonely at times, and that her artistic expression is wasted on me. I really do love her giftedness for creating welcome and making home such an inviting place. I know I should communicate and validate this value more frequently than I do.

5. I snore (so I'm told) really bad. Need I say more?

Much of the tension within a marriage, it seems, is simply one spouse trying to communicate to the other what the marriage is costing him or her. And usually, unfortunately, such "conversations" are filled with intense emotions so couples don't really hear each other. Instead, it's common for mates to go on the defensive in these heated moments, attempting to deflect the blame for their pain back onto the other. The beauty of this spiritual intimacy exercise we're suggesting is that when a spouse shows the ability to actually write out what the marriage costs his or her mate, there is a welcomed sense of feeling heard. "Ahh . . . he actually gets this"; "she understands me!"

Let us assure you: Even if you can't change the pain of the rub, you will feel more deeply connected because you feel understood. And feeling understood is a close cousin to feeling loved. Sometimes simply feeling understood is enough—enough to get through the times when the loving feelings just aren't flowing.

Another benefit of this spiritual intimacy exercise is it helps couples to see a picture of the wholeness of the relationship—the complementary aspect of the rub. A new awareness of what we would have missed without the rub of our individuality takes root. A picture of the "holes" God covered in our personalities by bringing us together begins to take form. For instance, in our case, we would have missed God's good plan to make much more whole two less usable people. When Valerie writes, Steve does the detail editing. When Valerie decorates, Steve makes sure the painting is done evenly or the wallpaper is hung straight and trimmed precisely—perfectly, in fact! Steve has opened up to Valerie a wide world of replenishing relationships and joy in people. Valerie has exposed Steve to antiques, art museums, theater, and relationships based on mercy, not simply good times. Finally, this aspect of the exercise forces us to think in new patterns towards each other.

Surprise. We are good together.

Though sometimes we still disagree and get caught up in the frustration of the rub, we also realize there's a richness in our relationship because of our differences. We're learning to celebrate our differences. We are rich with each other! We have a deep conviction that God was very good in bringing us together.

One couple described how they dealt with the rub in their relationship. They've always had friction within the marriage concerning punctuality and tardiness. He was punctual. She ran late.

Sunday mornings are less tense for Virginia and Redford Williams these days. Nothing has changed about Virginia's tendency to run late for church services. Her husband still doesn't quite understand what takes so long to get ready. "The difference is I stopped getting on her case," said Redford Williams, a physician and director of the Behavioral Medicine Research Center at Duke University in Durham, N.C. "Now I sit back and wait, maybe pick up a book. I'm not cursing and speeding on the way to church."[2]

The Williams's marriage has refocused away from changing each other to downplaying the negatives. The hostility and conflict that tear at intimacy have been relegated to a more appropriate perspective in light of all that is good about their relationship. Nothing has changed, but everything is very different.

Part 2. Gratitude: the Spotlight on a Couple's Blessings

The second part of celebrating the differences in your marriage is to express gratitude. We realize this may seem difficult; some would say even unreasonable.

One couple could not believe that they were to take this awareness of each other's costs in the marriage and use it to articulate their gratitude.

"Gratitude?" they looked at us blankly. We knew what they were thinking. It sounded overly simplistic! Our prescriptive exercise seemed way too shallow for their deep and difficult marriage problems.

"Yes . . . gratitude." We continued undaunted. "And begin by writing out the specifics you appreciate about each other, about your life together, about the increasingly mature couple you are becoming."

"But, what do we write?" It was apparent they still didn't believe this would help their marriage, which they are convinced is more twisted than anything that's walked down the aisle since Adam and Eve!

"Well, what is good about your life together? There must be something."

Silence. Finally, the young wife reluctantly offered this: "Well, he is really good with the children. I know I can depend on him to take care of them when I'm gone."

The silence resumed. Our eyes bored holes into the young husband, exposing his reluctance to take his turn at "playing this game."

"OK! Andrea is a great cook. Every night she makes incredible meals for our family. My mom was never that consistent in that area."

Andrea began to warm to his praise. She delivered the next statement right to Jon's face. "I'm grateful that you try to work through our problems and that you just won't give up, even when it just seems so hard. You're a bulldog, not only in frustrating ways, but in good ways too."

Laughter. Jon was feeling some understanding now. He was warming to the exercise. "I appreciate your sensitivity. I know I act like I think you're too emotional sometimes, but the other side of that coin is that you are tender and kind—especially toward me when I often don't deserve it."

As we watched them experiencing their own meltdown toward each other, we were reminded that a grateful spirit works wonders in the life of a marriage. Writing out gratefulness lists on occasion—together or alone—will enable couples to notice more of the details of God's blessing in their lives. As we continue to mature, as our spiritual formation develops even more fully toward receiving God's love and grace and then, in turn, extending that to each other, we are increasingly able to celebrate this perspective: that we are God's good gifts to each other! We recommend you begin a gratefulness list of your own.

THE ROLE OF GRACE

The Difference Between Denial and Grace

A couple of comments about steps two and three in this spiritual intimacy exercise we're suggesting. Some may wonder about accepting and even celebrating the differences when someone has acted without respect, even cruelly, in the marriage. What is the role of grace? Are we advocating living in denial? No. Denial refuses to admit there is relational tension.

"Denial comes from an internal preoccupation with avoiding pain," wrote Timmen Cermak in *A Time to Heal.* "Denial prevents us from seeing things that make us too uncomfortable."[3]

What we are advocating is grace. Grace in this context is extending the unmerited love you have personally received from God to your spouse as well. God's grace, seen in His love, is a "stooping down to embrace that which is worthless. His love is a free unconstrained decision to love sinful man; it is therefore a sheer and unqualified miracle."[4]

In other words, grace acknowledges there are problems, there are frustrations, there are great irritations and limitations, but chooses to balance the downside with the perspective that much is also worthy and right in the relationship. Grace chooses to remember what is good and tames our unattainable desire for human soul mating with the reality of God's perfectly suited love. Grace acknowledges the rightness

Spiritual Intimacy Exercise 3
Smoothing the Rub

This exercise is intended to move couples beyond merely tolerating their spouses to appreciating them. It will not eliminate the rubbing friction of differences in the marriage. But it will cause each partner to accept, even celebrate, the differences and thus lessen the effects of the rub. It involves a three-step process.

First, identify the rub. Recognize where the friction is in your marriage. Whether it is a difference in temperament, personal habits, interests, preferences, or some other area, you must identify the rub before you can deal with it. Usually the marriage will have one major difference, not multiple difficulties. Remember that by definition the rub is one aspect of your spouse that is largely unchangeable.

Second, accept the rub. Because the rub can be changed little, learn to accept it rather than try to change or "fix" the other person. This will require altering your perspective and learning new ways of relating to the differences between your spouse and you. Since we can become heavily invested in our own viewpoint, it may help to talk with someone who can bring a fuller perspective. Consider an understanding friend, able to emphasize the positives he or she has observed about the relationship; a caring pastor, who can remind you that God is to be our soul mate; a skilled counselor, equipped to direct you toward the realistic expectation for changes to yourself (rather than impossible expectations for changes in your spouse). Finally, when it comes to learning acceptance, don't forget the most important resource of all: Ask God for His supernatural grace to accept your spouse with the same love with which God accepts you.

Third, celebrate the other person. To go beyond identifying and accepting the rub to celebrating it may seem impossible. It can occur, however, when we recognize the whole cost of our marriage and respond with gratitude for the marriage and our mate.

This final step requires grace-filled love. Love that celebrates your partner's differences begins in prayer (see step two), but it is fleshed out when *we count the cost and respond with gratitude.* You will make two lists. First, count the cost; focus on what it has cost your spouse to be married to you. List on a sheet of paper at least five things. Then read your list to your spouse. This will humble you and make you appreciate your spouse more, which leads to the final part of this exercise. To express your gratitude, write out what you appreciate about your mate. The list will include positive traits, skills, and habits, as well as appreciation for your life together (see pages 118–19 for examples from Jon and Andrea's life).

✳   ✳   ✳

of God's plan for wholeness in the relationship. Grace resists ego's demands for change and instead learns to accept "as is" unconditionally —the way we all need to be loved in the end. Grace celebrates God's goodness in filling our individual personality "holes" with the "wholeness" of the other.

The grace to accept each other is grounded in the understanding that we are to offer to our mate that which we have received unconditionally from God. "Accept one another, then, just as Christ accepted you, in order to bring praise to God" (Romans 15:7). There is a maturity implied in this kind of married life together. How the world needs to see the difference Christ makes in a marriage of disparate individuals.

How Far Is Too Far?

How far should grace be taken in a relationship? Farther than most of us think. Really much, much farther. But can it be taken too far? Yes, grace without boundaries can lead to abuse. If there's a long history of insensitivity to each other's feelings, or if one or both partners are relationally obtuse (like the husband who demanded sex three times a day from his young wife, or the wife who refuses to take personal responsibility for her persistent emotional outbursts), then professional help may be necessary to rediscover where center is in a healthy relationship.

Working through boundary issues is very important, but it requires that couples play fairly with each other. And sometimes a referee is needed to help bring fairness into the relationship. How can one know when help is required? Outside help is almost always needed if one or both of the following conditions exist: (1) Either spouse is in continual emotional pain; or (2) the marriage stops functioning—that is, you have few or no meaningful conversations, communicating with each other literally ceases, sexual relations become nonexistent, or intimacy at any level is avoided. Any of these conditions indicate that you probably need to find outside help.

A Discipline of Grace

While some couples may benefit from outside help, most married people would benefit greatly by simply demonstrating more grace toward each other. In his classic devotional *My Utmost for His Highest*, Oswald Chambers wrote,

> The Holy Spirit reveals to me that God loves me not because I was lovable, but because it is His nature to do so. He commands us to show that same love to others by saying, . . . "love each other as I have loved you" (John 15:12). . .
>
> I should look within and remember how wonderfully He has dealt with me. I may get irritated because I have to live with an unusually difficult person. But just think of how disagreeable I have been to God! Neither natural love nor God's divine love will remain in me unless it is nurtured. Love . . . has to be maintained through discipline.[5]

The next time the "rub" threatens to capsize your feelings about your marriage, stop in your tracks. Instead, turn in your mind from negativity to what is honorable and positive in your relationship. Remember the apostle Paul's instructions:

Finally, brothers [and sisters],
whatever is true,
whatever is noble,
whatever is right,
whatever is pure,
whatever is lovely,
whatever is admirable—
if anything is excellent or praiseworthy—
think about such things. (Philippians 4:8)

Offering affirming words can be powerful, even humbling. But they are a key part of showing grace as we accept and rejoice in our spouse. During a difficult time in Steve's life, I sensed the Holy Spirit prompting me: "Valerie, tell Steve how much you appreciate him. Let him know that you don't take for granted his going to work every day! Thank him for the home he's given you and the lifestyle he provides for you."

Soon I tried these new-to-our-relationship words. This was virgin territory for me, and the words came out haltingly and self-consciously, unsure of themselves. Here was admittance of my real need of this man. Here was humility that owned up to my deep dependence on (not just my entitlement to) his care. Here was admiration and appreciation and gratitude. Here was recognition of God's goodness in our lives by bringing us together. How would he respond? Would he think I was being overemotional and shrug me away?

I said those words and felt emotionally naked for a few moments. Then an amazing thing happened. Steve's response was warm and wonderful! My sincere words sparked the beginning of a meltdown between us. I could see his body change before my eyes. There was a physical lowering of his shoulders, as if his spirit had lightened, taken a much-needed sigh, and relaxed. His pressures were not in vain after all. He was loved and appreciated.

With those simple words, sincerely meant and stated, we began a whole new healthier chapter in our marriage. He shared with me at a later date that he never feels more loved by me than when I express my appreciation and gratitude. We've learned that when we're on the receiving end of gratitude it not only makes us feel more loved, but prompts us to be more loving as well. Expressing gratitude also indicates that a spiritual rebirth is happening in a relationship.

We are determined to discipline our hearts to remember that there is something more important than throwing each other's egos to the ground and wrestling out a short-term win. There is honor in how we choose to treat each other. There is a growing respect for each other and for God by how we play this game of marriage over the long haul.

With a grateful heart and with God's help, we all can learn to celebrate our differences in the light of God's love.

Afterimage

"Never forget. Only selfish people have problems in marriage."

(Advice from Dad Burton to both of us sometime in the mid-seventies)

8

About
Kings
and
Queens

*H*ow we wish Scripture had recorded some of Adam and
Eve's more intimate conversations for us. In the years after their banishment from the Garden of Eden, did the first husband
and wife fight about how to raise their children? Were they verbally affectionate with each other? What did they talk about at night before
they fell asleep? Would we recognize shades of our own marriages in
their ancient exchange of words?

It seems possible. And we wonder if, like many couples today,
Adam wanted to be king and Eve wanted to be queen.

Recently our suspicions about wanting to lord it over each other
were confirmed by an ancient and fascinating piece of oral history: a
conversation estimated to be more than two thousand years old between a husband and his wife. It was handed down by filids, the highly
honored Irish scholars who, before writing was developed, preserved
knowledge by chanting from memory known history. The couple may
have lived more than two millennia ago, but the "who's on top?" tone
of their discussion has a familiar contemporary sound.

Ailil, the king of a province in Ireland is musing to his queen, Medb, about their life together:

> "It is true what they say, love: it is well for the wife of a wealthy man."
>
> "True enough," replies Medb, the queen. "What put that in your mind?"
>
> "It struck me how much better off you are today than the day I married you."
>
> "I was well enough off without you."
>
> "Then your wealth was something I didn't know or hear much about—except for your woman's things, and the neighboring enemies making off with loot and plunder."[1]

Medb is put off with Ailil's high tone. She reminds him that she is the daughter of the high king of Ireland and of his daughters she was the "highest and haughtiest":

> "I outdid them in grace and giving and battle and warlike combat. I had fifteen hundred soldiers in my royal pay, and the same number of freeborn native men, and for every paid soldier I had ten more men . . . !"
>
> [She does not stop.] "My father gave me this whole province of Ireland . . . you are a kept man. . . . It still remains that my fortune is greater than yours!"
>
> "You amaze me. No one has more," shouts [the king], gesturing grandly, "than I have, and I know it!"[2]

That very night they take inventory of their possessions. Jewels and pots and finger rings, cloths of purple, cloths of stripes and checks, rams and herds of pigs and stallions are all paraded out to make the point. Tit for tat they argue until their marital discord leads them dangerously close to civil war with each other.

WHO'S ON TOP?

Who's on top? Who brings the most to this marriage? Whose life has been most improved by this arrangement? Who got the better deal?

Oh, sainted ones, those of you who have never had such a self-serving thought enter your mind about your own superior contribution to your marriage—we salute you! But for us, the couple who lives together as king and queen of their own small turf, we admit to such conversations. Thankfully, the filids are not recording the words of our marital discussions for generations to come. We are much more content having control of snitching on ourselves than having been observed and spied on. So our parading of "your life is so good because of me" occasionally sounds like this in our home.

Steve, as he folds the laundry—laundry that is white, white, white as the freshly fallen snow, thanks to his two washings (one in cold water with soap, the second in hot water with both soap and bleach):

"You know, Valerie, I don't know many women whose husbands take care of them the way I take care of you. I mean, what would you do if something ever happened to me and you married again? Believe me, no one else would treat you this well. Do you realize I spoil you so bad? You are aware, I hope, that you're the quintessential kept woman!" The king of clean struts his stuff for his wife to admire. He knows he is good. Does she appreciate it?

Then there's Valerie, who stands back admiring a room she has pulled together with practically no money; using instead garage sale acumen and plenty of artistic resourcefulness—all along thinking that Martha Stewart has nothing on her:

"Steve, I shudder to think how you would have lived if I hadn't married you. Sterile, that's what it would have been. Functional and plain. No art. No pillows. No luscious color. No antiques with their cracked and worn wood patina. Do you realize what I bring to your life? Do you know where you would be without me? Drab, drab, drab!" The queen of the artistic perspective has peacocked her stuff, hoping for admiration from her husband. She knows she is good. She wants to be sure he gets the full impact of their quality of life because of what she does for him.

OTHER THOUGHT-PROVOKING QUESTIONS

We admit to having had these embarrassing-to-report conversations on occasion. We've never taken them very seriously—just a kind of marriage bantering and playing with each other's minds. Each of us wanted to be the exalted leader, to receive the praise and unquestioning admiration from our mate. But a while ago when a couple asked us a question, one that had been posed to them by their own marriage counselor, we paused.

Who Does the Most Accommodating?

Their question to us: "Who does the most accommodating in your marriage?" Their counselor was trying to help them find center, a place of balance in their marriage. They knew the answer in their own marriage. They had discovered that some of their problems were caused by too much accommodation by one of them. They were working on leveling out the playing ground in their relationship.

"Who accommodates the other the most in your marriage?" The question made us think.

"Hmmm . . . well, we both accommodate each other," was our almost immediate reply. Initially we felt good about our mutually agreed upon response, assured that the other had not quickly claimed the accommodator role. But in the week that followed we began to observe our lives through the grid of "Who does give the most?" We each noticed how accomplished the other was at receiving. We observed our small, previously overlooked sacrifices—who makes the popcorn at night when we're both tired, who answers the phone when neither of us wants to talk, who walks outside in their bathrobe in the morning to pick up the paper for the other, who bends or flexes the most to please the other, who runs to the store for the quick purchase when we've run out of something, who gives the final go-to-sleep-afterwards back rub. In other words, who's on top and who's not.

By the end of the week each of us had concluded, "I'm the one most taken for granted." Both of us were convinced that the other had gotten the "deal of the century" in this marriage.

Why Keep Score?

There is obviously a danger in thinking of marriage as if there is a scoreboard with his points and her points. But there also is a danger in not examining this relational dynamic in the light. Why? Because this frequently overlooked marriage dynamic holds a powerful capacity to destroy a couple's desire for spiritual intimacy with each other. A wife may feel that her husband forfeits his credibility as the home's spiritual leader because he communicates selfishness about who is "most important" in the relationship. However, it goes both ways; the husband who feels used and unappreciated—just someone to support his wife's lifestyle and selfish agenda—will have little desire for spiritual vulnerability and intimacy. *Lead her spiritually too?* He doesn't want to further accommodate her in any other way.

In the beginning of this book, we compared the condition of spiritual intimacy in a marriage to the role of the miners' bird deep down in a coal shaft. If the shaft starts running out of air, the bird struggles and, if not attended to, dies. The bird's struggle and impending death signals an alarm. The miners know by the condition of the bird how safe the mine is. Similarly, when a marriage is in trouble, spiritual intimacy is typically the first thing to die. It's not uncommon to resist praying with someone who's taking advantage of you. Also, there's a tendency to avoid real vulnerability. If spiritual activity together becomes rote, boring, or empty, consider it a warning sign: Take a look at the real condition of your relationship. Many married partners seem to be more comfortable faking physical intimacy with each other—having perfunctory sex without a positive emotional context—than they are faking meaningful prayer together or sharing their souls with each other. Going through the motions of spiritual intimacy in a troubled marriage is just too uncomfortable for most people to attempt.

Avoiding spiritual intimacy is often the first telltale symptom of a marriage in trouble. And because self-exaltation and exploitation can undermine our own desire for spiritual intimacy and lead to avoiding such intimacy, it's important we take a bald, honest look at one-sided accommodation in marriage.

Who Is on Center Stage?

Who is most accommodating to whom in your marriage? Or said differently, who is your marriage most about? Who is center stage? Not sure? Then the answer to these questions might help: Who determines how a vacation is spent because of the more pressing need to "restore"? Who sets the agenda? The one who is center stage is the one on top, choosing the superior position and being most accommodated.

Through the years, we've observed many marriages that seem to be built primarily on one-way accommodation. This one-sided approach is sometimes apparent in the marriages of accomplished Christian leaders, businesspersons, and executives who have tremendous personal charisma and possess the drive, passion, and skills that can build successful ministries, businesses, or organizations. A common perception from the outside looking in is that life with such a person must be terrific with all the success, prestige, and sometimes money. But the spouse is often unseen, even unappreciated. Ironically, when problems in their relationship become public, the all-too-often unfair conclusion is that this "superman" made an unfortunate marriage choice.

Look a little closer. For the strong pastor or male executive, the marriage often is almost completely about him. His wife bends to accommodate his schedule, his "more important" life, his needs, his pressures. By choice or not, he is her ministry. When it comes to their "shared" life together, everything from cutting the grass to dealing with the children, "their" life becomes her responsibility so that he can be freed up to focus professionally.

After a busy day that has been about them and their workplace—accommodated by staffs and assistants to acomplish projects—they return home and the pattern continues. They expect their wives to continue to serve them, yet they do not reciprocate in love for all the wives' help in rearing children and keeping the home. The result? Some of these women feel sad or end up in counseling, wanting out of their marriages. The marriage is not about the wife at all. Many such women have never discovered their personal gifts or developed their own goals or interests. All their energies have gone into their husbands. For each wife, her personal development has practically faded off of the life screen; yet most onlookers feel she is lucky and unappreciative about the wonderful mate God has given her.

Or consider a marriage where a husband or wife has not resolved a problem with workaholism. Whether or not the couple is Christian, most likely someone at home is paying an enormous price. It is the sin of the more dominant life force bending the lesser to near nonexistence. Often, in such cases, workaholics have absolutely no clue what they have done to their spouse or family. They are oblivious to the attitude of entitlement.

One-sided accommodation has many subtle dynamics. Sometimes the most powerful person in a marriage is the one who is least well. Instead, the one who is the more fragile is constantly served and protected—even catered to. A weak marriage partner can require enormous life energy, focus, and attention from the healthier spouse. Who is such a marriage really about? Who, for instance, gets lost in the marriage of a workaholic or an alcoholic? Often it is the healthier spouse. Where is center—the balance point—for such couples? Some cross the line between appropriately catered to and self-centeredness run amok. Some move beyond an appropriate level of having their needs met to displaying an attitude of selfish entitlement: "I need and deserve care."

Spiritual intimacy is very difficult in a marriage, in fact, nearly impossible, when one person has faded from the marriage dynamic.

"In order to be intimate, you need a self. Otherwise, getting close to another person always offers the possibility of being swallowed up by that person."[3]

REVEALING STORIES FROM
THE LEWIS AND CLARK EXPEDITION

The best-seller *Undaunted Courage,* about the Lewis and Clark expedition, includes a detailed account about the condition of the Indian women whom the two explorers met. In his journal (complete with original spellings), Meriwether Lewis glimpses into the pre-Christian world of marriage:

> The Shoshones treat their women but with little rispect, and compel them to perform every species of drudgery. They collect the wild fruits and roots, attend to the horses or assist in that duty, cook, dress the skins and make all their apparel, collect wood and make their fires, arrange and form their lodges, and when they travel pack the horses and take charge of all the baggage; in short the man does little else except attend his horses, hunt and fish. The chastity of their women was not held in high esteem. The men would barter their wives [sexual] services for a night or longer, if the reward was sufficient. [4]

Later, Lewis contrasts the slightly better treatment of wives among the Pacific-dwelling Chinooks with the Shoshones and other plains Indians:

> They did not hold their virtue in high esteem "and will prostitute their wives and daughters for a fishinghook or a strand of beads." As with other Indians, the women did every kind of domestic work, but, unlike other tribes, Chinookan men shared the drudgery. Even more surprising to Lewis, "notwithstanding the survile manner in which they treat their women [the men] pay much more rispect to their judgment and opinions in many rispects than most Indian nations; women were permitted to speak freely before them, and sometimes appear to command with a tone of authority."[5]

BIG SINS . . . LITTLE SINS

Most who read Lewis and Clark's reports about the treatment of wives among the Indians are immediately repulsed by the bartering of their women's sexual services. Today, Christians consider sexual unfaithfulness as one of the big sins in marriage. Pastors preach about it from their pulpits. Volumes have been written about infidelity from the viewpoint of Christian values. We teach our children that Christianity is linked to sexual purity. Sexual promiscuity is a "biggie" on the Christian ranking charts of sin.

The "Little" Sin of Using Our Spouse

But does it seem strange that we are less put off with one-sided accommodation of women to men, or vice versa? Is the usage of a marriage partner for drudgery and selfish advantage not also sin? Indeed, this blatant "swallowing up" of someone else is not unlike the pre-Christian values among husbands and wives in these early American tribes.

That we are not as disturbed by the everyday condition of life for these spouses as we are by sexual promiscuity—that we fail to be aware of the parallel ways we "civilized" Christian couples treat each other in our own marriages—suggests that we are more pagan and less reflective of Christian values than we realize. Interestingly, the tribes considered more civilized were those that had learned a degree of honor about sharing the drudgery and honoring their wives' opinions. The same progress is apparent today. The more "Christian" a couple is in their attitudes to each other, the more attention they tend to pay to the everyday issues of workload and mutual input into decision-making.

Beware the Pagan Marriage

Is it possible for a couple to have a marriage that is professedly Christian but pagan in values and practice? The disturbing answer is yes. That is the precise definition of a Christian marriage before spiritual rebirth—simultaneously Christian and secular. Such a marriage may passionately avoid overt sins, but ignore how the marriage is actually being lived out in the "everydayness" of the relationship. Does this couple relate to each other any differently than those in neighborhood marriages where Christ is not professed? Are the more subtle sins addressed or receiving any attention at all? In Scripture Solomon cautions couples, before it's too late, to "Catch . . . the little foxes that ruin the vineyards" (Song of Songs 2:15).

All Sins Matter

It is a major oversight to think that only the "big" sins matter in marriage. Couples who want to enjoy an optimum marriage must realize that spiritual intimacy can be lost through inattention to any sin. Satan's arsenal of weapons against Christian marriages is subtle; he intends to destroy our relationships by subjecting husbands and wives to being "nibbled away by the minnows" much more than being "swallowed by a whale." We may ignore the more subtle sins of insensitivity, everyday neglect, or usage of a marriage partner that, over time, can shred our relationships, thinking we're safe because the shark of sexual infidelity isn't swimming in the sea. But we actually are swimming with many little piranha.

It's not uncommon for a marriage without an actively engaged Christian spiritual dimension to be reduced to one partner being on top while the other is diminished by one-sided drudgery and sacrifice. This pagan attitude is the curse of the Fall, and it's unknowingly lived out in the daily grind of many "Christian" marriages. "One of the goals of Christian marriage," writes author and counselor David Stoop, "is to 'reverse the curse' of the husband ruling over the wife and the wife seeking to overthrow his leadership."[6]

MAKING CHRISTIAN MARRIAGE A VISIBLE SIGN OF GRACE

The Christian home is potentially differentiated from secular culture by its marked sacramental approach to daily life. In other words, the Christian marriage is to be noticeably, visibly, apparently different than the other marriages on the block. This is what we mean by a sacramental marriage. A sacrament (known as an ordinance in many churches) is a Christian observance full of symbolism. Milne has defined a sacrament as an "an outward and visible sign of an inward and invisible grace."[7] In a sacramental marriage, a husband and wife relate to each other in such a way that there is a visible sign of an invisible grace.

For instance, "in the sacrament [or ordinance] of baptism, the water is the outward and visible sign of the inward and invisible grace of the 'washing of rebirth,' the forgiveness of sins [which has taken place earlier], the union with Christ in death and resurrection, and entry into the body of Christ. In the sacrament of the Lord's Supper the outward and visible signs of the bread and wine represent or symbolize the inward and invisible grace of the benefits of Christ's death to those who believe, the spiritual 'feeding upon' Christ and the communion with the people of God."[8]

So too, in Christian marriage there is a sacramental relationship between the visible, obvious, apparent way a couple lives out their lives together that symbolizes the love that God has for the body of Christ. Thus, by design, the Christian marriage *looks* much different from others. This difference should be clear and obvious.

What a high calling and challenge—to represent in our marriage relationship a picture to each other and those around us what God's love is like. In a spiritually rebirthed marriage, providing care is seen as a sacred ministry, an expression of sacramental living, a willing service to each other and God Himself. Do you clean house and prepare meals and receive such care with appropriate thanks and understanding that something of holiness has been ministered to you? Or does it all pass by you because cultural and gender expectations have dulled your awareness of the privilege of sacramental living and your call to holy living with each other?

BALANCING OUR ROLES

Too often the Christian principle of wifely submission has been taught without equal emphasis on the balancing principle of male servant leadership. And too often male servant leadership has been taught without the balancing principle of honoring the woman, who also is a servant with skills and gifts. The call in the Scriptures—the very sacramental principle behind marriage—is mutual submission, mutual care, and mutual honor. Without such an understanding, Christian homes are in danger of practicing one-sided accommodation, which can drain a marriage of all possibilities of real spiritual intimacy and trust.

Admittedly, it can be very difficult to view our own marriages in a clear light. Who accommodates whom? Who serves the other more? Does our relationship have a sacramental element to it? That's why we were interested in some feedback our older son, Brendan, gave us about our own marriage recently. (A graduate student in psychology, Brendan is soon to be married and therefore has been increasingly interested in such dynamics.)

"I've observed that Dad is usually the leader, running the show, but it seems that if Mom becomes passionate about something, Dad will accommodate her strong opinions. Mom's vote definitely matters."

Brendan's observations confirmed our own understanding of where we are on the "who's on top" scale. Interestingly, though, in all these years of our marriage, neither of us can remember an incident where we disagreed to the point that Valerie submitted while uncomfortable with a decision. Of course, we don't always agree; we debate issues frequently—even heatedly. But we have always managed to mutually bend to each other's interests, needs, and passions in an egalitarian fashion. One of the most differentiating "visible" signs of a marriage being lived out Christianly is the noticeable grace that honors Christ by "submitting yourselves one to another" (Ephesians 5:21 KJV). In a relationship where the husband and wife revere Christ and care for each other, where they each show a sincere commitment to flex and stretch to the dimensions of God's love, issues of submission become less central and less defining. A spiritually rebirthed marriage will be ruled by the law of love, marked by mutuality, and operated under the ultimate headship of the husband—when it comes down to that.

HOMES OF MUTUAL RESPECT

As a child, Valerie often visited a friend whose mother she loved deeply. The mother was not a Christian believer, but interestingly, she was the most nurturing of all the adult women in Valerie's life at that time. This mother expressed a remarkable focused attention on her children and all of their friends. Valerie and her siblings were always welcome in her home. "She loved to feed us; her enjoyment of us was clearly obvious."

All was well—until her husband arrived at the house. Then the home was totally transformed. Even though this woman appeared to lavish the same attentive care on her husband, he was terrible to her. As soon as he walked through the door, the situation soured. Sometimes he'd be in such an obvious angry snit that he refused to speak to anyone. Meals were never good enough for him. He emotionally polluted that home with his snideness, his volcanic angry venting, and his childish demands.

How sad that the nurture and care this gracious woman brought into her home was taken for granted. She was not appreciated. She was verbally and emotionally abused. It makes us ill to think of what her life must have been like from day to day.

Unfortunately this situation that Valerie observed as a child is not unique to non-Christian families. Christian homes should be homes of respect. It's disturbing to realize how many "Christian homes" live out this after-the-Fall lifestyle as well.

Spiritual Intimacy Exercise 4
Practicing Visible Signs of God's Grace

As husbands and wives we can become intentional in serving the other. This develops a sacramental marriage, where both partners demonstrate "outward and visible signs of inward and invisible grace." Such outward actions are signs of God's grace working in our relationships with our spouses.

Here are several ways you can demonstrate God's grace in your marriage, as husband and wife:

- He learns to cook a few special meals so she can have a break from the kitchen, without the expense of eating out.
- He learns to give a real massage, without expecting sex afterwards.
- He gives up all wife jokes and instead begins to quote her or ask for her opinion publicly.
- He takes on some regular responsibility for housework. Cleaning the bathrooms. Scrubbing the floors. Vacuuming. Laundry. And he does these chores without being asked.
- She washes the car, a job usually on his list.
- She learns to give a real massage (longer than two minutes), complete with body oils and soothing music.
- Rather than going to bed, she stays up and keeps him company on a night he has to work late at his desk.
- Questions like, "How can I best help you? What would you like for me to do for you?" are asked regularly. Maybe he's been wanting a new tool or piece of sports equipment. Wouldn't he love it if his wife took the initiative and it just showed up some night when he arrived home? Why wait for an anniversary or your wife's birthday so that you can make "mileage" on a purchase or a special favor? Is there something she would love to receive or have done and it's within your reach to make it happen now?

The previous suggestions assume certain "traditional" roles and reversing them. But service can cross other relational dynamics as well. Here are some other suggestions that a husband or wife can practice:

- Whoever usually mows the grass is surprised upon returning home to find it has already been done.
- Someone cleans the fridge and fills it with the other's favorite food.
- Whichever partner typically calls for the baby-sitter is delighted to find that the other has already made the necessary arrangements for the sitter this time.
- Errands are run together or for each other.
- Crises are managed so that each partner has the luxury of emotional care from the other. That means the mate who is more frequently "in crisis mode" is learning to become even and emotionally strong, in order to be ready to provide support and care when called upon.
- The partner not primarily responsible for earning the family income displays special care toward the finances. He or she affirms the primary breadwinner for the contributions that sustain the family. This involves concrete expressions of thanks and appreciation and not overspending at home (which could incline the primary wage earner to work even more).
- Consider gifts of time. How might you free up some time in your spouse's busy schedule? Is there something you can do that will give him or her some downtime instead?

✳　✳　✳

A CALL FOR TRANSFORMED LIVING

Defying the Fall

The "outward and visible" signs of a marriage are telling. A Christian marriage is defined not by its stated theological stand alone, but also, if not more, by its outward and visible indicators. In a rebirthed state, Christian marriage becomes a symbol of God's love, a living testament to the difference Christ makes. In a sense, the rebirthed marriage defies the Fall.

What light does the following passage from *The Message,* Eugene Peterson's dynamic paraphrase of the Scripture, shed on the small, everyday treatment of how married believers treat their partners?

> So here's what I want you to do, God helping you: Take your every-day, ordinary life—your sleeping, eating, going-to-work, and walking-around life—and place it before God as an offering. Embracing what God does for you is the best thing you can do for him. Don't become so well-adjusted to your culture that you fit into it without even thinking. Instead, fix your attention on God. You'll be changed from the inside out. Readily recognize what he wants from you, and quickly respond to it. Unlike the culture around you, always dragging you down to its level of immaturity, God brings the best out of you, develops well-formed maturity in you.
>
> I'm speaking to you out of deep gratitude for all that God has given me, and especially as I have responsibilities in relation to you. Living then, as every one of you does, in pure grace, it's important that you not misinterpret yourselves as people who are bringing this goodness to God. No, God brings it all to you. The only accurate way to understand ourselves is by what God is and by what he does for us, not by what we are and what we do for him. (Romans 12:1–3)

Spiritually intimate marriages are models of transformed thinking. The Christian marriage should be unlike pagan relationships not only in its faithful sexual practices, but also in the way the partners reflect God's value of mutual service and humility toward each other. And while it's not abnormal for one person in a marriage relationship to receive more of the relational focus, Christian couples realize that whoever may be "on top" at one time must become spiritually sensitized about his or her position of privilege.

Also, he or she must fully comprehend the potential abuse of such a position. Such an understanding requires conviction; any awareness of abusing one's position will require repentance. Repentance means a turning away, or being repulsed by anything that is not pleasing and honoring to God. Though repentance is a key ingredient in one's salvation experience, it doesn't end there. Repentance is to be an operative response in our lives as God's Spirit sensitizes us to areas in need of realignment to His purposes.

In our relationships, Crabb writes, "We must remember that the essence of holiness is other-centeredness, a worshipful love of God and love for others that motivates sacrificial care for them."[9]

A Painful, Personal Example

Several years ago the Lord convicted me about being the focus of our marriage energy too much of the time. Although we both accommodated each other, I began to sense that too much of Steve's life energy was directed at caring for me. This growing conviction about the potential darkness I was starting to see inside myself encouraged me to take this question, "Who accommodates whom most in this marriage?" out of our marriage closet and examine it in the light of my own Christian beliefs.

My first uncomfortable twinge came with a long look back—an afterimage that needed years and maturity for me to interpret accurately. As our two sons became increasingly involved in competitive sports during their teen years, I couldn't help but think of their father at this age. Steve was a gifted athlete, the pride and joy of his parents and extended family. At 5 feet 7 inches, he was a surprising wonder, especially on the basketball court, with a deadly long shot (before the arrival of the three-pointer), speed, and charisma as well. He was an impact player, always the leader of his teams. In college we all loved watching him play.

After our third year of college, we married. We were both still in school and both of us worked multiple jobs—but Steve in particular worked constantly to support us. He reluctantly decided on his own to give up basketball. Then in a strange ironic twist, he got a job driving the basketball team bus to most of their away games. For that entire season, which would have been his last, he sat in the bleachers eating his heart out watching the other "boys" his age play. Marriage to me had benched him permanently.

I'm embarrassed to admit it, but at that time I just thought, *Well, that's life. If you're going to be married, you have to give up being a boy.*

But now as a woman, a woman with adult sons, it hurts me to think about what that exceptionally talented and skilled young athlete gave up for an unnoticing, unappreciative new wife. I regret that now. Worst of all, I feel ashamed when I remember that I was so blasé, so ungrateful for his sacrifice.

Why? We were married. Care was expected. Wasn't I entitled to financial provision from my husband regardless of what it cost Steve?

In the years that followed, I expected Steve to "meet my needs" in other ways. Through the death of my parents and a frightening bout with cancer, it seemed like I had the corner on crisis. The emotional leaning always went one way—towards him. He could never fall apart. I was too busy doing that, taking all the turns at bat in the crisis department. And of course, he was always there. A solid, positive anchor. My confidence builder. My most loyal supporter. The man who can make me feel better just by walking into the room.

But when did he ever have the luxury of being emotionally cared for? Was it fair that most of the emotional care was going one way, always in my direction? At one point in our marriage, when he was experiencing inordinate professional pressures—and I started experiencing wifely insecurities about the future—Steve was reduced to saying to me, "Valerie, this is not about you. This is my crisis." In other words, "I can't carry my problems and your insecurities about my problems too. I need you to carry your own weight and help me get through this."

Initially I was put off with what I considered a distancing stance. But I finally began to hear what he was trying to say. I took a closer look at what he was facing—it was an impossible predicament and he was stuck. Now was the time he needed my support and encouragement.

God was speaking to me and my heart began to soften, then break for Steve. I needed to turn away from my female-role entitlement attitude—that is, to repent. I had taken so much for granted. How I wished I could financially support us for awhile. I couldn't even equalize the support emotionally in our marriage. I would never be able to handle as well as he does the details and everyday pressure areas of our lives.

I began to pray regularly: "God, show me how to honor this good man You've given me. How can I lighten his current heavy load?"

A SPIRITUAL ISSUE

"Who's on top?" in a marriage is a spiritual issue. Spiritual Intimacy Exercise 4 (pages 136–37) helps us to find the balance in our marriage, so that neither a king or a queen lords it over the spouse. The exercise implies we are to be proactive—to initiate practices that show greater sensitivity and a commitment to mutual service and care. Initiating the exercise will make you more intentional in serving your spouse and demonstrating God's grace.

Remember, our outward, visible care for a spouse is never demeaning but honoring to both God and each other. It is a sign for all who may notice that we are different—a couple living out our Christian beliefs in full view, overcomers of the Fall, new creatures, transformed in our minds and hearts to be His image-bearers in this sin-sick world.

It's true that you may never be able to "even" the accommodation scoreboard in your marriage totally—one partner may always be more needy, or more dominant, or in more demand. But you can even the "playing field" of marriage by expressing your gratefulness to each other. Don't take each other for granted. Notice the small daily sacrifices. Appreciate the precious gift of shared life you bring to each other. Say "Thank you . . . I appreciate you . . . I'm so grateful to you" more frequently. Notice the laundry, the paychecks, the gifts of time and energy and effort. Defeat Satan's minnow attacks by refusing to ignore the "small" sins of selfishness. Instead, turn opportunities for selfish actions into noticed, holy, sacramental expressions of God's love. In doing so, we turn from being kings and queens into being servants, like Jesus.

LOVE IS NOT SELF-SEEKING

Scripture says that "Love is patient, love is kind. It does not envy, it does not boast, it is not proud. It is not rude." Often when I write I have a coffee mug with those and other 1 Corinthians 13 verses painted on its outside next to my computer. But curiously I noticed that love "is not self-seeking" (verse 5) is missing from the mug. And for good reason perhaps. What does "love is not self-seeking" mean? Even the Bible commentaries disagree about the interpretation of those words. But when "love is not self-seeking" is put through the marriage grid, in light of this tendency towards selfish one-sided accommodation, it doesn't seem like much of a stretch to suggest that it might mean:

- Love does not seek its own . . . agenda.
- Love does not seek its own . . . care.
- Love does not seek its own . . . focus.
- Love does not seek its own . . . entitlement attitude.
- Love does not seek its own . . . growth at someone else's expense.

Immature love is selfish love. Mature sacramental love spurns staying on top; instead, it actively seeks ways to even the playing field in a relationship. Years ago Valerie's father told us this differently—in a more blunt way: "Never forget. Only selfish people have problems in marriage." We shrugged off his advice as an oversimplification of the marriage dynamic. But recently we've been understanding that it is closer to the truth than most of us who are married would like to admit.

The call to show God's grace in a sacramental marriage is a call to service—and a call to overturn all self-seeking love. It is another way to develop spiritual intimacy toward each other and toward God.

If you've been trying some of the spiritual intimacy exercises we are suggesting in this book, we hope you are noticing that the bird of longing for spiritual intimacy is perking up, starting to chirp a little, beginning to feel more at ease. The groundwork is being laid in your relationship for a decidedly more spiritual approach towards each other. You may not be there yet, but you could be well on your way to having the marriage you've always wanted—a marriage, given the distinctives of your personalities and unique issues, that is on its way to becoming "as good as it can be."

Afterimage

And above all, we promise to work toward an ever-growing love so long as we both shall live.

(From Steve and Valerie's wedding vows of June 20, 1970)

9

When Things Spiritual Seem Dull

C ouples in marriage counseling often are asked the following question: "So, what do you do to have fun together?" Counselors know that a couple's level of enjoyment can indicate the degree of satisfaction in their marriage. We wonder if God might want to ask a similar question to Christian spouses who have dulled-down spiritually, "So, what do you do to enjoy Me together?" It follows that if you enjoy your spiritual process with each other, then you are more apt to pursue spiritual intimacy together and eagerly seek God.

The focus of this question may seem strange for some whose relating to God has been primarily intellectual, those who perceive accessing God primarily as a kind of "thinking our way into heaven."

SPIRITUALITY: A MATTER OF RELATIONSHIP

Perhaps this tendency to intellectualize God (as opposed to experiencing a relationship with God) explains the *Westminster Catechism's* clear emphasis on the relational focus of spirituality. "The chief end of man," according to the Catechism's summary, "is to glorify God, and to enjoy him forever." How can we capture this relationship with God?

It's true that without some Bible knowledge we may fail to "glorify" God through our misunderstanding and lack of awareness about how God has specifically revealed Himself to humankind. Yet some warning labels are appropriate for those of us who tend to become a little "heady" in our accessing of God or who think that traditional spiritual disciplines are the only route to revelation.

In *My Utmost for His Highest,* Oswald Chambers issued this warning:

> Your god may be your little Christian habit—the habit of prayer or Bible reading at certain times of the day. Watch how your Father will upset your schedule if you begin to worship your habit instead of what the habit symbolizes. We say, "I can't do that right now; this is my time alone with God." No, this is your time alone with your habit. . . . Love means there are no visible habits—that your habits are so immersed in the Lord that you practice them without realizing it.[1]

Bruce Milne, a professor of theology at Spurgeon's College in London, gives these additional guidelines and cautions for daily Bible study:

> As well as innumerable blessings [in personal Bible reading] there are also dangers in this practice; for example, an almost superstitious, "horoscope" attitude can develop whereby the portion to be studied each day is detached from its biblical context and forced to yield some hidden, special message relevant to the reader's immediate situation. . . .
>
> We also need to beware of developing a legalistic attitude whereby we presume to earn God's blessing because we have fulfilled our daily devotional obligations, or of becoming burdened with a sense of guilt and the feeling that "today is bound to go wrong" if we miss our Bible study time. The sovereign God of glory does not depend on our feeble religious exercises for the operation of his purpose in our lives, or to protect and bless us in his grace.[2]

NEW WAYS TO ACCESS GOD OUR FATHER

Perhaps considering some new paradigms about accessing God would help all of us.

The disciples learned the importance of being open to new thinking patterns from Jesus Himself, following His resurrection. They had fished all night yet had caught nothing. In the morning, Jesus appeared, standing on the shore, though the disciples did not recognize Him at first.

> He called out to them, "Friends, haven't you any fish?"
> "No," they answered.
> He said, "Throw your net on the right side of the boat and you will find some."
> When they did, they were unable to haul the net in because of the large number of fish. (John 21:5–6)

They did not know it was Jesus, but weary and unsuccessful, they were willing to try a new approach. It worked. Understand, we are *not* suggesting that you stop fishing—or stop reading your Bible, or discontinue praying together, or cease your devotional time alone or with each other. No. Don't abandon any of these practices even if you haven't been very successful so far. Indeed, keep trying.

But we do want to suggest that there are additional ways to learn to enjoy God together. Furthermore, the benefits to your marriage may become abundant, more than you can haul in all at once because the possibilities are so many. Yes, other approaches that help you learn to access and relate to God also count.

CREATIVE APPROACHES TO VIBRANT SPIRITUAL INTIMACY

In this chapter, we will suggest a variety of ideas to sharpen the spiritual side of your marriage, to replace the dullness with a sharp edge. In a sense, these are ways to "cast your net on the other side" of the spiritual intimacy boat, to provide you and your spouse with some positive experiences and success at enjoying God together. The ideas that follow all can be part of another spiritual intimacy exercise. In fact, Spiritual Intimacy Exercise 5 (see pp. 154–55) summarizes these creative ways to revitalize spiritual intimacy in your marriage.

Seeing God in Creation

Through the illumination of the Holy Spirit, God reveals Himself through Scripture; that's true. Biblical revelation is vital to knowing God. But He also reveals Himself through what He has created. This is called general revelation. The awe and wonder we feel in the presence of a beautiful sunset or majestic snowcapped mountain is a close relative to worship.

When you see a beautiful sunset and your response is to put your arms around each other and say, "Look at that . . ." if you'd simply add, "Ah, God!" you will have just entered into an experience that is more than an appreciation of nature. You will have acknowledged God as the creator and sustainer of this universe and of your lives. That's worshiping together.

Try an *Ah, God!* weekend together. It's an intentional time set aside to heighten awareness of God's great goodness. Everything seen, experienced—the smells, the colors, the textures of life, the people around you, the relationships you encounter—all go through the grid of *Ah, God!*

What you might normally pass by without noticing, when put through the grid of *Ah, God!* becomes a reminder of how precious the gift of life is.

Worshiping in this fashion may help you notice a child, perhaps your own, finding a caterpillar and letting it crawl across his little hand, causing him to laugh with joy at the encounter. Maybe you'll come upon a child sharing his ice cream cone with his dog, or a neighbor's yard filled with autumn colors, or a mountain range from the window of an airplane that you otherwise would not have been able to see. An *Ah, God!* perspective could help sensitize you anew to His presence in this wonder-filled world He created, which displays His glory and power.

Seeing God in History

History is another of the ways God reveals Himself to mankind. Sometimes it's only in the long look back that we come to understand how God has worked out His good plan for this world. By taking an *Ah, God!* weekend in an historic place it may enable you to capture that "long look back" perspective and let the significance of God's good involvement in this world soak in.

Valerie and I celebrated our twenty-fifth wedding anniversary on a battlefield—literally! We had planned this dream-of-a-lifetime (three weeks in France) trip together months in advance. On the self-driving tour we had purchased, part of the package included two days exploring the Normandy beaches, where allied troops landed during a pivotal invasion of World War II.

Frankly, we were not initially very interested in this leg of the journey—neither of us being World War II buffs—but it was "tacked on" to our tour through the Loire Valley and on our way to Giverny where we looked forward to visiting Monet's home and gardens. We stuck to the planned arrangements. We weren't expecting much from it and were somewhat disappointed to have to spend our anniversary at a war site. (Although that might not be as inappropriate as it sounds!)

But surprisingly, we became quickly intrigued and overwhelmed. As we toured the museums, reading the accounts of the sacrifices in young human lives made on those beaches, understanding for the first time the genius and courage of the Allied leadership, and realizing afresh the evil of Hitler, we were deeply touched and cried. We walked across narrow strips of intact beachhead, land bridges just wide enough to step one foot in front of the other, surrounded by huge, pocked bomb holes. In the evening we watched the fog rolling over the channel into the American cemetery as we stood among the thousands of white grave markers—both crosses and Stars of David. For the first time in our lives, we shed tears for members of our parent's generation as we saw their young faces, taut with fear, newsreeled into eternity. We cried for their parents and the price they paid for freedom, for all who had lost their lives to evil—the Jews, the Poles, the French. For the world's pain we cried.

What was happening to us? It was an unplanned *Ah, God!* experience.

Ah, God! Thank You for showing up in the history of this world. Thank You for intervening against the spread of rampant evil. *Ah, God!* Thank You that our parents and their parents understood that some causes are worth dying for.

That unanticipated powerful on-site history lesson was a new-to-us general revelation of God's earthly activity. And it was amazingly and surprisingly moving. God can reveal Himself to you through a look-back perspective one weekend at an historical setting, whether in your state or traveling across the country or across the ocean.

Seeing God in Genuine, Alive Worship

God is with us. What Bible-believing Christian could disagree? But most of us could do more thinking about what activities make us increasingly aware of God's presence, where we're more alive to Him or more apt to cry out "Ah, God!" in laughter and enjoyment of life. *Ah, God!* Those are the activities or experiences worth pursuing as a couple. Think about it. Such situations should be built into your lives . . . together!

One setting that often generates a sense of God occurs in special times of worship together. We encourage your spouse and you to experience joyful worship and a renewed awareness of God's presence. But what do we mean by worship? What we're suggesting can be experienced corporately inside the walls of a church or can be found outside in nature, in your home, in a prison or war zone—any place where God is honored can be experienced as holy ground.

The English archbishop William Temple has given a powerful, revealing definition of worship: "Worship is the submission of all our nature to God. It is the quickening of conscience by His holiness; the nourishment of mind with His truth; the purification of the imagination by His beauty; the opening of the heart to His love; the surrender of will to His purpose."[3]

That definition of worship describes the many possible responses to God that we experience in authentic worship. Ask yourself, *What activities, or pursuits, or state of mind bring out these responses in me as listed in that definition?* In other words, ask yourself:

1. What could we do together as a couple that would draw forth the responses of submission or surrender to God in all parts of our nature—not just in our heads? What specifically causes us to submit our eyes, our emotions, our energies, and relationships —all of ourselves—to God?
2. What increases our sensitivity to sin and makes us more keenly aware of God's holiness?
3. What expands our minds to God's truth? What nourishes our thinking and turns us into seekers of God's truth?
4. What increased creative activity causes us to open to beauty, open to love—especially the beauty and love of God?
5. What motivates us to seek God's will for our lives above all else?

Why not begin to seek God along such avenues that encourage these kind of responses? As you answer these questions in terms of your marriage, you may discover possibilities for pursuing spiritual intimacy in places and activities that up to this point you've been overlooking, or haven't even considered as potentially "spiritual."

An *Ah, God!* day, or weekend, or week might bring about such responses. It is one of the best returns on the investment you can make together as a couple.

Seeing God Through a Prayerwalk

The term *prayer-walking* is probably new to you, yet the tradition of husband and wife walking and praying with God is hardly a new idea. It's as old as Eden. It was during God's walk through the Garden of Eden in the cool of the day that Adam and Eve hid among the trees. Scripture doesn't specifically say that walking with God was Adam and Eve's normal pattern, but we can infer that God normally would have been joining them during His walk in the garden. Only on that particularly sad day, their sin made them feel guilty so that they became "no-shows."

Of course, simply walking together as a couple is always a practical way to spend healthy connecting time with each other. But now go to the next level: share in an intentional "prayerwalk."

Praying and walking are a natural combination. A couple can take along a prayer agenda, some specific Scripture texts, and their voices to sing—if they have enough privacy or, lacking privacy, courage! Keep your eyes open as you pray and remember, there's no need to whisper. Talk right out loud—to God, together.[4]

Valerie and I have discovered that there's just something about the physical moving that helps jog our prayer thoughts. Typically we'll walk for about forty minutes. That means we have quality uninterrupted time to be with God and with each other. There are no phones or doorbells to answer; we don't have to worry about fielding important questions from the kids—we're out of range! Nor do we need to rush the process or stop praying because of pressing issues calling for our attention in our home offices. When we're out walking, we're too far away to notice!

But what do you say for forty minutes, especially if you've never been able to think of enough words to fill five minutes? You don't need to spend all the time talking. Sometimes you can simply listen. Enjoy God's presence. Quiet your spirits and listen for His agenda. With a little practice—and without many words or a formal prayer agenda—a couple can experience the nudgings of God to pray, or act, or respond in any number of ways while they are prayer-walking together.

Even if you never said a word while you were prayer-walking but used the time to experience God's love—to listen for His words of care about you—you will find that prayer-walking is a beneficial tool to experiencing God together.

Seeing God Through New Forms of Corporate Worship

Sometimes you can see God in a whole new light by experiencing a kind of worship experience different from the one you're familiar with at your own church. Besides the private husband and wife worship so important in your marriage, new kinds of corporate worship can drive you closer to God. Here are some ways to do that.

Make an opportunity to attend an inner-city church and worship in a black, Hispanic, or Asian church. Or if that's normal for you, visit a suburban Presbyterian worship service some weekend. If your church experience is mostly liturgical, try a more contemporary worship service and vice versa.

Please don't misunderstand us. We're not encouraging church-hopping, nor are we wanting to undermine your faithful participation in a local fellowship of believers. It's just that every type of Christian worship highlights a different aspect of our great and mighty God. Some worship styles are joyful, others more somber; some include a wonderful usage of historical language, while others are more modern or entirely spontaneous. Now and then, be open to another approach for a change. Leave your critical spirit at home and go as a seeker, a student of fresh perspective about the truth of who God is.

In addition, consider attending special area-wide meetings for worship and spiritual instruction. If you ever have an opportunity to attend a citywide Concert of Prayer—by definition an interdenominational, intergenerational, cross-gender, cross-racial area prayer event—grab it! Wherever the body of Christ gathers in large numbers—a denominational meeting, a Graham or Palau crusade, or a Concert of Prayer rally —you will likely get a glimpse of what heaven will be like when the whole body of Christ will gather someday to worship our Lord together. According to Revelation 7 that will include "a great multitude . . . from every nation, tribe, people and language, standing before the throne . . ." praising our God forever and ever! Get a sneak preview of heaven and participate with Christ's larger body in worshiping and seeking Him together in this spiritually stimulating manner.

Seeing God Through a Gratitude Journal

A gratitude journal can sensitize us to God's involvement. Too often we miss God's regular participation in our lives. It doesn't have to be. God surrounds us with an ocean of blessing; we are practically swimming in His goodness, and all we can think about is that we might drown! Begin a gratitude journal where you write down that for which you're grateful in your marriage and your lives. Be sure to include some grateful responses to God as well.

To get started, try listing three to five new items every day. You can do this together, or if you want, separately. After a period of time, say the end of the month, review your journal together. You'll be amazed at the value of this exercise!

During a period of uncertainty, having a grateful perspective is truly healing. Recently Rich resigned from his position even though he had no new job waiting. With two kids in college, it was the most expensive time of Sue and Rich's lives; their financial backup systems were thin at best. On one level it seemed like a crazy thing to do; but the couple agreed that God was leading them to step out in faith. Still, they felt the financial pressures and were worried about the days ahead. One evening they decided to take a walk to a small lake near their home.

Soon they were sitting by the lake. In silence the couple watched the geese paddle by for some time. Then Rich began:

"Even now we have good lives."

"Even if you don't find a job, our children bring us great joy," Sue chimed in.

"Yeah, and it's not like one of us died. We still have each other," Rich responded. Their spontaneous litany continued.

"We still have our home."

"We still have our friends."

"God still loves us and we know He'll help us."

"The fact is, we're rich. We're rich in family."

"We're rich in relationships. We're rich in each other."

"We're rich in God! Why are we worrying and wrecking this day?"

Now consider the impact of recording those words of thankfulness in a journal. Expressing mutual gratitude—creating a gratitude journal —will give needed perspective to flesh out the spiritual truth of the song that proclaims:

And now let the weak say I am strong,
Let the poor say I am rich,
Because of what the Lord has done for us,
Give thanks.[5]

Spiritual Intimacy Exercise 5
Ways to Welcome God into Your Marriage

In a variety of ways, husbands and wives can enjoy God's presence in their marriage. If your marriage has a spiritual dullness, here are several approaches for developing spiritual intimacy with God and each other.

1. *Reveal God in creation.* Have an *Ah, God!* weekend together. Take time to see God in Creation: His sunsets, mountains, oceans, flowers, animals, even bugs. During the weekend try to become aware of God's greatness and goodness in what you see and experience, from the smells and colors of life to the people around you.
2. *Visit an historical site.* God reveals Himself in history. During a local weekend trip or an extended vacation, travel with your spouse to an historic locale and find God's footprints there. As a couple, discuss what you learn about God there: His love, mercy, willingness to let men and women choose (and perhaps fail), etc.
3. *Take a prayer walk.* Take along a prayer agenda, some specific Scripture text, and walk some path—just the two of you—praising, singing, and talking about God. It's a practical way to have connecting time with God and each other.
4. *Visit other churches to participate in new worship experiences.* A church worship that differs from yours is not necessarily inferior, just different, and its style can open your spouse and your eyes to new truths about God. Change can remind us that worship can have both joy and awe, spontaneity and order, rich language and common, contemporary words.
5. *Make regular entries in a gratitude journal.* Include entries about events, traits, and qualities in your marriage and your lives that make you grateful. Include grateful responses to God.

6. *Observe God's creativity and grace among animals.* Whether observing fish at the city aquarium (or during a snorkeling trip) or playing with puppies at a pet store, your spouse and you can enjoy God's animal kingdom and recognize the beauty, fun, and creativity God displays in surrounding us with living things.

7. *Participate together in service projects.* The projects may benefit the church (being a worker or teacher in the nursery or Sunday school, for instance) or the community. You could even take a short-term missions trip. Your service will glorify God and see Him at work in your lives and the lives of those you serve.

Other ways you can access God, bringing Him closer to you and your marriage, include: (1) join a small group study, (2) meet with a prayer and accountability partner, (3) sing worship songs and hymns together, (4) pray with your spouse with your hand resting on him or her, and (5) share with each other insights from your current reading. These approaches are discussed in this chapter.

✳   ✳   ✳

Seeing God Through the World of Animals

Weird is wonderful. Even animals reflect the delightful creative spirit of God. God must have enjoyed making them. The cavorting otter, the sociable monkey, the armadillo that looks like it was made up of spare parts from someone's garage—they all attest to God's playfulness and delight in creating.

Here's another suggestion: Go diving or snorkeling with the intent of viewing the sea life from God's perspective. Or go to a pet store and play with the puppies. Enjoy. God went to a lot of effort to populate earth with such pleasures. When you get back home, plan to do something fun and creative together. In the spirit of playful creativity, remember it doesn't have to be productive or have a point. It only needs to be expressive, fun, and a way to reflect and honor God's creative process in your lives. Celebrate beauty and color and texture and God's goodness for providing us with so much that is pleasurable in this world.

Seeing God Through Service Together

Here's another possibility: Get involved in a kingdom project together. Volunteer to work in the church nursery, or help out in Sunday
school, or teach a kids' club. You might use your home as a place to
extend hospitality to older folks, college students, foreign exchange
students, missionaries, visitors to your church, your unchurched
neighbors. Are you a gourmet cook? Can you bake a mean batch of
cookies? Think, "How can we offer to God what we enjoy doing?"

When your spouse and you participate in some service project,
you connect with each other, having unique, special experiences that
bind your lives and memories together while serving God. Such joint
projects are opportunities to present your bodies in "spiritual service
of worship" (Romans 12:1 NASB).

Force yourself to think out of the box. If you've never worked in a
homeless shelter or a city mission, you might be surprised how enjoyable it is to serve people who need a helping hand. It really is not de-
pressing. If you can hammer a nail straight, think about volunteering
for an organization like Habitat for Humanity or a nearby housing
project. Have a garage sale and give the proceeds to a worthy ministry.
Pick a project, any project, and honor God by doing it together.

A wonderful stretch in the service area for most couples would be
an international short-term missions trip. If the opportunity ever arises, don't pass it up. The body of Christ is diverse, broad, and very hos-
pitable in other parts of the world. Cross-cultural experiences can be
enriching, humbling, and eye-opening. Valerie and I have been on
many short-term missions trips overseas, and we cherish the rich exposure God's people worldwide have brought to our lives. Here are
just two of the afterimages we recall: A prayer meeting in a Haitian hut
by lantern light where we were given the only tattered hymnal to hold
as a gesture of their Christian hospitality towards us; the godly couple
whose wedding we attended, who had waited fourteen years to save
enough money for a Christian wedding. We participated with them as
we paraded through their village behind them, banging pots and
singing hymns as a testimony to Christian marriage.

We still see the Christian joy of people we have met in dozens of
countries—faces that most Americans would think had no reason to
be happy. We still hear the exuberant singing, the prayers in other lan-
guages that reached right down to our souls.

God is never boring overseas! American Christians benefit greatly through exposure to God's people around the world. It forces us to take another look at our values, our devotion to God that has cost us practically nothing, our spoiled complacency, our materialism, our acquisitional lives.

Seeing God Through a Small Group Study and a Prayer Partner

For almost twenty years we have been involved in small groups together. This has been very valuable for our individual spiritual growth as well as our growth as a couple. We've never studied the topic of marriage in one of these group settings, yet we have learned a lot about ourselves as a couple. How often have we said to each other, and heard other small-group spouses declare, "I didn't know that. You never told me that."

A small group of committed, growing spiritual friends provides the kind of safe place for married partners to mature in their faith and towards each other. Together they can draw close to God. Whether studying Scripture together comes easily for you or not, involvement in a small group with a study agenda, regular meeting times, and lively spiritual conversation will only boost your mutual sharing and the maturing of your spiritual processes as husband and wife. This is a healthy learning arena that will help to nourish your minds with God's truth.

One variation of the group is a personal prayer partner. I've had the same personal prayer partner for more than ten years now. Accountability is a large part of the dynamic between Doug and me. If things are getting a little rocky at home, often Valerie and Claudette, Doug's wife, will suggest to each other, "Don't you think the guys should be getting together a little more frequently?" What they are seemingly kidding about is the truth we have learned through the years: A prayer partner can definitely improve your marriage.

Having a trusted, caring friend carrying your concerns and bringing God into the dynamic through prayer is a tremendous life asset. Plus a prayer partner who knows you well can often be the catalyst for the "quickening of conscience" in response to God's holiness. For ideas on developing a prayer partnership, read *Two Are Better than One,* an excellent resource by David Mains and Steve Bell.[6]

One of our friends reports that her most intimate spiritual friend asks her at times, "I've been listening to what you say, but I must ask you, is your response one of walking in the light?" Ouch . . . and thank you as well.

Seeing God by Singing Together

When was the last time you were lullabied to sleep by an old hymn, spiritual song, or scripture chorus? We suspect you were about two years old if you ever did enjoy such a life luxury. Steve and I are both musical and enjoy singing together, but you don't have to be musical to enjoy this comfort with each other. You just have to understand the potential of this mutual experience, and you'll want to try it together, even if you can't sing on pitch, sound like a bullfrog, or can never remember the words and end up humming every time.

The music can lift our spirits and turn our focus back to where it should be. The words can remind us of key spiritual truths about God, His Son Jesus, and our relationship to the Father and the Spirit. Scripture choruses immerse us in God's Word; old hymns, such as "And Can It Be" and "Holy, Holy, Holy" teach us theology while comforting our souls.

We learned firsthand of the comfort that comes from being sung to. When Valerie's father was dying—he had been mute and seemingly without mental capacity for more than four years—Valerie sang to him. When she stopped he would grunt, indicating he wanted more. It was the only communication between them during that long period of his illness. It was finally a way to ease his suffering. As he struggled with his last breaths on earth, Valerie sang and sang, tears running down her face, nose running, heart breaking. She was honored to be able to say good-bye to him in that way.

Since learning of that very personal expression of care, we have used it in our own marriage. With arms around each other we'll sometimes sing of God's love, or heaven, or peace. We just curl up with each other and sing out our faith. It's a little like Frederick Buechner's definition of faith, "whistling in the dark" except for us it's "singing in the dark." Why should childhood have the corner on the luxurious blessing of being lullabied in the arms of someone who loves you?

"Ah, God! Life is sweet and I am nurtured toward loving You more all the time!"

Seeing God Through an Old Prayer Form

Of course, God reveals Himself in prayer, and many couples find spiritual intimacy as they pray. Some couples hold hands as they pray. But we also recommend a more formal, yet connecting position for prayer. The person who is praying can lay hands on the other's shoulders or head as he or she prays. There is a ministerial feel to this position, a position of invoking God's blessing through intercessory prayer. By taking such a position towards a spouse in prayer, the priestly function of care for each other is symbolized—and the power of touch gives comfort and support.

One weekend when I had to leave home for a speaking engagement I was finding leaving particularly difficult. I needed a blessing from Steve and a sense of affirmation about God's calling on my life. I asked Steve to pray with me. Sitting at the piano bench together side by side, he laid prayerful hands on me, one hand on my shoulder, the other on my head, then he prayed.

Our black cat, Tar Baby, sat on her hind legs on the other side of me and put her paws in the "laying on of hands" position on my opposite shoulder. My leaving even had the cat's blessing that weekend! What more affirmation could I want?

We can't promise your pets will be cooperative, but we know you'll benefit from the sense of ministry to each other you'll find through laying hands on each other as a way of blessing your spouse.

Seeing God by Sharing Books and Other Reading Material

Make a date to share with each other the things you've read or are currently reading. You can snuggle together in the love seat, in front of a fireplace, or perhaps on a well-lit, screened-in porch at night. Then tell each other what you have been reading about God, spiritual issues, or married life.

We often surround our bed with books and magazines for an early-to-bed evening of reading, or we visit one of those coffee shops that encourages loitering. In any of these settings or by our fireplace, we enjoy sharing the things we're reading.

Augustine said that "All truth is God's truth." That means that some things that aren't technically "spiritual" may still lead to truth about God. Don't be afraid to branch out to other areas of interest—art, history, biographies, great literature. Include some good Christian books along the way as well and you will be prepared for a wonderful time together as you integrate God's truth into your relationship.

As you gather reading material, consider reading newspapers and magazines with a pair of scissors nearby. Cut out jokes, cartoons, snatches of information, editorials, and columns from newspapers, pictures of beautiful locations, homes, children . . . *anything* you want to share with the person you love.

Most of all, such a time will provide a natural way for you to discuss your opinions, your growth edges, and what you're processing spiritually as you interact and reflect on the offerings of thought you bring to each other and examine under God's light of truth.

THE QUEST FOR CONNECTION

But, some may wonder, do these suggestions really count as spiritually intimate activities? We can answer that legitimate concern by reviewing our definition of spiritual intimacy: *Spiritual intimacy is the satisfying connectedness that occurs when a husband and wife learn to access God and experience Him together on the deepest levels.*

What do we mean by the "deepest levels"? Must that always imply a spirituality that is intense and theologically profound? The Old Testament writers suggest spiritual closeness will include great joy. (See, for example, Psalm 51:12; Isaiah 35:10; 61:1, 3.) The psalmist looked forward to drawing close to God's "dwelling place." "Then will I go to the altar of God, to God, my joy and my delight. I will praise you with the harp, O God, my God" (Psalm 43:3–4). Zephaniah called upon the people of Israel to have great joy:

> Sing, O Daughter of Zion; shout aloud, O Israel! Be glad and rejoice with all your heart. . . . The Lord your God is with you, he is mighty to save. He will take great delight in you, he will quiet you with his love, he will rejoice over you with singing. (Zephaniah 3:14, 17)

Measure your hearts. What makes them leap before God with joy? What brings you closer to God and to each other? What puts an edge back on a spirituality gone dull? Pursue those things and come to know Him together as the psalmist knew Him, "God, my joy and my delight."

Afterimage

Just months after we were married, Valerie asked her mother, "Does sex ever seem strange to you?" Mom Burton's response:

"Just remember, Sweetie, we didn't invent sex. God did. And therefore, it must be a good gift."

(Sometime in the fall of 1970)

10

Sexuality and the Spiritually Intimate Marriage

*T*o our great delight, our family was able to attend the 1996 summer Olympic Games held in Atlanta. We had not bought tickets in advance, so we were fortunate, once we arrived in town, to obtain some of the last ones available. They were not big venue tickets, like basketball, gymnastics, or track and field, but at two hundred dollars plus a pop, such seats were out of our financial league anyway. For $19 each, we happily made our way to the semifinals in badminton doubles.

Like most Americans, we weren't too acquainted with organized badminton tournament play. We certainly had no idea of the devotion of its fans, particularly among the Asian countries. And so, amazingly, we found ourselves swept up into the bleachers surrounded by enthusiastic Asian fans—a family of blonds in a sea of Korean students. This was fun. The students graciously equipped us with flags, hats, and instructions to smile for the Korean television crew, who were recording our American enthusiasm over their team for the folks back in the homeland.

We had better get this right. The success of our American foreign diplomacy with Korea may rest with the Bells making a favorable impression!

Unlike its stuffy, pretentious, country-clubbed cousin tennis, badminton encourages fan participation. "Ahh-wah!" one side of the arena yells together in one voice at the precise microsecond the shuttlecock is returned. The volley back is articulated with an enormously threatening, "Sss-aah!" from the fans of the returning side's team.

And then we heard this curious chant: "Give honor! Show respect!"

We were fascinated and totally charmed. What a foreign concept to our American sports battle cries of, "Smash them! Show no mercy! Nail the quarterback!"

On the drive home our family recalled the scene, speaking much about how honor and respect are practically foreign concepts in so many areas of American life. Interestingly, our conversation next turned to sex. Our entire family agreed that there is no area more obviously distanced from honor and respect than the area of sexual relationships between American men and women.

That is why in this chapter we've chosen to consider sexuality in terms of spiritual intimacy. We believe marital sexuality deserves to be recaptured from secular thinking and replaced on the pedestal of honor and respect, for distorted or dishonoring sexual experiences can hinder spiritual intimacy, and loss of spiritual intimacy likewise can hinder our sexual expression to our spouse. Where do sex and romance fit in the lives of spiritually intimate couples?

This is only one of many questions we can ask. Does sex belong to the spiritual realm or to the physical? And what about romance—do romantic feelings and actions indicate the level of a couple's intimacy? Does romance have any connection at all to spiritual intimacy? What can we realistically expect from sex and romance? Where do they belong in the scheme of a Christian marriage?

ROMANCE: ALL THE TIME?

Romance seems a lot like the celebration of Christmas. Months ago as we dismantled Christmas and packed it in boxes, storing it in the attic for another year, we remembered the joy of early December, decorating our old 1917 vintage prairie-style home. We had placed electric candle lights in every window, forbidding winter's early pouty gloom. We had draped the festive garlands and trees with shiny glass ornaments that shouted color to a world given to premature graying at 4:00 P.M. (too early for the approaching night, at least as far as we are concerned).

Curiously, there comes a day, a week or two after Christmas, when we know it is time to pack away the decorative fancies and simplify. We yearn for regular and plain. Our eye editor screams, "Make space. De-clutter. Organize." All the Christmas treasures that were once sentimental now seem like a lot of excess baggage. Finally, we're ready for winter's gray cold and can face it without the Christmas props.

In fact, we want it. To the degree that we welcomed the Christmas season's cheer, now we are relieved that no one will be dropping by gift boxes of fat-laden cookies and calorie-popping chocolate. We could not withstand that temptation year-round. We need breathing room from the romance of Christmas. That joyous, but intense holiday as center front stage in our lives has become too much.

We've noticed the same feelings about sexual romance. While it is wonderful to be swept off your feet now and then, we could not function with romantic fantasy consuming all our everyday energy, passions, and time. We pull it out of its packing for a weekend away or a cold winter's morning warming each other in front of a blazing fire. But shiny-eyed romance gets assigned to the attic so that the more orderly pragmatic season of love—the winter of paying bills, doing laundry, the time for cleaning bathtubs—can have the energy it deserves. We never worry that Christmas won't return, nor do we worry about romance. We know it can be pulled out of storage and into our lives with a little planning and intentionality from either or both of us.

It would be crazy to want the intensity of Christmas or romance every day. Hooked on holidays or hooked on romance would be a difficult addiction with which to carry on life.

But many people don't see it that way. Especially when it comes to romance and sex. Some view sex as the ultimate celebration of romance and expect it to provide a continual physical and spiritual high. When sex becomes the "drug" of choice, when you are "hooked" instead of in control, weird things begin to happen between a couple. Instead of experiencing more satisfaction, they often experience a dulling to each other and less fulfillment with sex in general. Just as holidays every day would decrease some of the sparkle and appreciation of the celebration, so sex at its ultimate intensity, as the primary focus of your relationship, would become less fulfilling and satisfying.

A SEXUALLY ABUSIVE MARRIAGE

A while ago a mother who had run away from her home visited us for the weekend. In very little time, we realized how emotionally spent this woman was. With one uncontrollable teenaged daughter bending the home to her own pubescent will and one disengaged husband who had absented himself from the scene, she simply could bear no more. She was welcomed in our home.

Soon she spoke with us about her current stresses; she also spoke about the breakup of her first marriage.

"He wanted to watch pornographic videos together. At first I went along with him because it seemed to heighten our sexual enjoyment. But our sex became more intense, painful, almost violent. I realized he was not making love to me, or even having sex with me, but using me as a way to vent his anger and frustration. In time he could not have 'regular' sex with me like we had when we were first married. I was really scared to stay with him. We finally called it quits and broke up the marriage."

Her husband's fantasy sex had destroyed his real relationship with his in-the-flesh lover. Normal sex with a real woman was dull, unsatisfying, an easy sacrifice to his god of the pornographic image. It's as if his desire for intense sexuality every day dulled his sexual receptors to the place that his enjoyment of sex was fully diminished. So was his relationship with his wife fully diminished.

Some of what enters into the bedroom of a husband and wife cannot be classified as anything less than sexual abuse. A few years ago, lawyers and spouses entered the debate about whether a wife can legally accuse a husband of rape. The answer, according to the courts, was yes. It follows that sexual abuse is not only possible but operating behind the closed doors of many marriages. Though the topic is too extensive for proper coverage in this book (and one we will leave to the legal experts to discuss), spouses can show physical disrespect and even abuse to their mates under the umbrella of "anything goes" in marital sex.

DIMINISHING RETURNS

During a recent jet flight, the man seated next to me opened up unusually quickly. When he learned I was a minister, he initiated a conversation about sex and marriage. He described the diminishing return on his sex life:

"Well, Steve, my first wife and I married when we were college students. We didn't know anything about sex. Everything was new and exciting, and during sex all of my thoughts were of her. Unfortunately, that marriage lasted only a few years.

"My current wife is a beautiful woman. But after ten years of marriage, I think of her during lovemaking very little. I am not cheating on her. But I seem to need to think pornographically or about other women in order to click with my wife these days."

This man seems to think that his difficulty in enjoying sex with his current wife is the natural result of his aging process. It doesn't seem to occur to him to consider that his admitted exposure to pornography and implied experience with many sex partners may have diminished and dulled his sexual sensitivity. Obviously, he was most satisfied with sex when he was more naive and enjoyed the capacity to be totally involved with his in-the-flesh wife. Years later, he has a beautiful wife but is deadened to her. How sad.

We shudder to think of the young men our younger son met while pledging a fraternity at a state university. In the end Justin did not join, partially because it was an open practice for some of these college men to bring young women up to their bedrooms, watch pornographic videos together, and have sex. Justin was appalled. We, too, are alarmed for these young men and women. What sexual extremes will they need in order to be fulfilled in their sex lives by the time they are forty or fifty? How much of their life energy will go into capturing that ever-more-illusive sexual high? And will any man or woman want them with all the sexual baggage they will be carrying by then? They are on their way, if not already there, to becoming sexual addicts—people who want it to be a holiday every day, at least sexually, and will sacrifice all other aspects of their lives to this god of the sexual high.

THE PROTECTION OF SPIRITUALITY

That's why we chose to include sex in a book about spiritual intimacy.

Take God out of the bedroom, ban Him from sensitizing the sexual thought life, and in time sex will be experienced as less than the wonderful expression God intended it to be. Sex belongs under the protection of spirituality.

Sex between a husband and wife is worth protecting, is worth putting into spiritual perspective, is worth considering within the framework of God's creative intentions for its expression. Only this way can we have the highest return on our intimacy investment with each other.

Connected As One

Sex between a husband and wife should connect them to each other. There should be an intimate awareness of everything about the person you are loving. Sex practiced with a spiritual perspective is as if the person you love has been put under a magnifying glass and you see him/her as greatly increased.

"And the two will become one flesh," the Scripture tells us (Ephesians 5:31). One flesh. That is the Christian perspective on sexuality. One flesh means not traveling separate roads of self-gratification by using each other. It means a coming together and experiencing sexuality as one unit. Crabb describes this as "Body Oneness," characterized by:

- Sexual pleasure between a couple who depend on God to meet their needs and are committed to being used of God in meeting each other's needs;
- Sexual pleasure that grows out of commitment to minister to one's spouse in the physical realm by giving maximum sexual pleasure;
- Sexual pleasure that provides a shared experience of sensual excitement and sexual satisfaction;
- Sexual pleasure that heightens each partner's awareness of their unbreakable bond.[1]

Christian marriages are like small sailboats clinging to honor in a cultural sea powered by inappropriate passions, lust without limits, and selfish uses of sexuality of the worst kind. Christian couples are in desperate need of spiritual images to help us navigate towards God and each other in a cultural sea gone wild over sexual gratification.

An Enhanced Relationship

What is Christian about sex? Professor Stanton Jones offers these excellent guidelines about sexuality that is framed within the context of a Christian marriage:

> Sex is meant to unite a husband and wife into one flesh. That means that while physical pleasure is important, it isn't the primary reason that God created sex. The sexual relationship is meant to build up and enrich your relationship.

Since my sexual relationship to my wife is meant to be a personal encounter . . . it should be "transparent." It should provide a window that allows me to see my wife clearly and emphasizes my love for her and her alone. We need to exclude anything that is "opaque," things that obscure our view of each other.

How can a couple engage in foreplay while watching a video of other people having sex and expect that to draw them together? That is really drawing other people into your relationship and it obscures, rather than enhances, your view of your spouse.[2]

That bears repeating. Through sexual relations, we are to enhance the view of *our spouse*. The primary reason God created sex is *to enhance a couple's relationship*.

How counter this runs to our culture's sexual expectations and obsessional focus on self-satisfaction during sex. Sexuality practiced for sexual gratification alone is sexuality that is precariously perched for disaster. People who make their own physical pleasure the focus in their marriage risk becoming users of each other (users of passion), risk denigrating a loved spouse into a sexual object (abusers of passion), or risk experiencing a diminished effect instead of an increased enjoyment of sex (dulled to passion). [3]

THE BLESSED MARRIAGE BED

A Gift to Give

A married person's sexuality is a gift of God that one can give to his or her spouse. The natural, pleasurable enjoyment of that gift is like the frosting on the cake of intimacy, but it is not the cake. A couple's increased connected relationship is the cake. The sexual relationship between a husband and wife should be the ultimate expression of care for each other. Sex is the ministry of physical intimacy.

And although it is "natural," the sexual relationship is also fragile. Sexuality can veer off course in many directions. Statistics reflect this reality. In our son's graduate program he recently learned that 10 percent of women who marry will be sexually nonresponsive. Other statistics reveal the pervasiveness of sexual abuse, indicative of the pattern that men and women have of abusing this gift of God.

God intended sex to be a passionate abandoning, a vulnerable celebration of relationship to each another. Sexual abuse, sexual avoidance, or sexual addiction all potentially destroy the sexual blessing God ordained to be present in marriage.

Boundaries: For Maximum Trust and Contentment

God is the pleasure creator. Not the pleasure spoiler. When He gives the parameters of fidelity, monogamy, and committed, loving sex, He is not a killjoy. He simply knows, as only the Creator could, how fragile our sexual wiring can be, and the necessary boundaries men and women must have in order to enjoy maximum trust, maximum vulnerability, maximum enjoyment. These "unalterable rules for living," captured most directly in the Ten Commandments, have, according to author Judith Couchman, "built the foundation for all that is moral and noble in the world. However, since their presentation, humanity has persisted in breaking God's rules, heaping trouble upon itself." Couchman adds:

> The Bible reminds us, "Love the Lord your God and keep . . . his commands always" (Deuteronomy 11:1). We don't readily grasp that God's rules are for our good. Instead of destroying individuality and enjoyment, His immutable laws protect us from harm, lead us into spiritual abundance, and grant us peace. For when we obey, we receive His blessing.[4]

Our sexuality is God's blessing. But use sexuality as it was not intended and it becomes a destructive weapon aimed at the very soul of our dearest on earth—our spouse.

FIVE SEXUAL COMMITMENTS IN MARRIAGE

How can a couple, desiring to honor God and each other even in their sexual relationship, find a framework for spiritual sexuality? The following five basic guidelines form a spiritual commitment with each other and with God. Such a commitment will help a marriage move toward spiritual intimacy.

1. Regard Sexuality As God's Gift

Commitment one is: "We will each view our sexuality as God's gift. Furthermore, I will strive to be sexually healthy so that my sexuality will be a blessing in your life." Taking care of each other's sexual self should be a couple's intimate ministry. God made you to be loved, and He provided married sex as a tool for that expression and you as the gift of that expression. Any attitude that views sexuality as unnatural or shameful, instead of a gift that God has given the husband and wife to enrich their love and deepen their commitment, has no place in the lives of spiritually intimate couples.

It can take some practice to get this right.

When we were newlyweds, Valerie had a rare heart-to-heart talk about sexuality with her mother. Talking about sex was unusual in those days, even with your own mother. But Valerie took the chance and confided in her mother that this new-to-her area of sex seemed a little "strange."

In a quick response that revealed more of her perspective on sex than a long theological treatise might have, Valerie's mother laughed and said, "Well just remember, Sweetie, we didn't invent sex. God did. And therefore, it must be a good gift."

In three sentences, Mom Burton introduced God into our bedroom and reassured a sexually immature daughter that there was nothing unnatural or strange about the physical relationship between a husband and wife. In fact, just the opposite was true. Sex is God's idea. It is holy ground between a man and woman. The marriage bed is a place to give and receive this blessing to each other. Spirituality belongs in the bedroom.

The second part of this commitment involves the desire to make "my sexuality a blessing in [my spouse's] life." Because a husband and wife are totally dependent on each other sexually, the sexual relationship between them is an area where power can become an issue. We must be careful not to remove that blessing by using our sexual power inappropriately or neglecting our mate sexually.

Sometimes wives withhold sex or simply refuse to enjoy sex or they take such poor care of their bodies that their husbands struggle to be aroused. Sometimes husbands never initiate sex but make their wives beg for their physical attention; other husbands simply satisfy themselves, leaving their wife sexually frustrated. Such misuses of one's sexuality can reflect rage, contempt, or indifference to their spouses and for themselves. Professor and counselor Dan Allender writes,

> Sexual dysfunction or compulsiveness is often a sign of undealt-with rage. . . . For example, a woman who has little interest in sex needs to admit that she is depriving her husband of legitimate intimacy and pleasure. But that fact will not increase her desire nor improve her sexual relationship, even if she forces herself to have sex. She must be willing to face that her lack of interest is a form of both relief (avoidance of unpleasant internal realities) and revenge (withholding intimacy and pleasure).[5]

A desperate woman confided in us about her husband's withholding of sexual pleasure from her. The only way he would engage her in a form of sex was to let her fondle his genitals between her knees (until he ejaculated). He would not satisfy her in any way; in fact he communicated his disgust with her every time they "had sex." Instead of experiencing acceptance and being found desirable, this woman was forced to experience her husband's rejection. Sex was the weapon of rage through which he was wounding her.

We need to honestly evaluate what we are really communicating to each other through our sexual attitudes. Sex that is used to bless each other will convey that the other is desirable and enjoyable, the object of our sexual arousal. In contrast, sex that wounds each other communicates disinterest, avoidance, and a user or abuser mentality.

The Bible is remarkably clear about sexual mutuality within marriage:

> The husband should fulfill his marital duty to his wife, and likewise the wife to her husband. The wife's body does not belong to her alone but also to her husband. In the same way, the husband's body does not belong to him alone but also to his wife. Do not deprive each other except by mutual consent and for a time, so that you may devote yourselves to prayer. Then come together again so that Satan will not tempt you because of your lack of self-control. (1 Corinthians 7:3–5)

Clearly sexuality is God's blessing and needs to be protected from any sexual attitudes, practices, or expectations that would destroy its blessing in our partner's life.

2. Practice Exclusive Sex

Commitment two is: " We will practice exclusive sex—both in mind and body." When sex is not reserved for only one person, the spouse is not showing commitment. There is a sense of betrayal and mistrust that will affect all future encounters.

During a plane trip, a woman friend of ours began a conversation with a young man in the next seat. They talked about the actor Christopher Reeve, a quadriplegic paralyzed after falling from a horse. The two talked about how Reeve's wife stayed with him through "better and worse." They admired his wife's strength during his subsequent paralysis.

The young man asked our friend this question: "Would you stay in your marriage if that happened to your husband?"

"Yes, I would stay," our friend answered. "And I believe my husband would not leave me if some catastrophe happened to me. We are committed."

"Not us," the young man confided. "We've already decided that if life gets too tough or something better comes along, say Kevin Costner came into our lives and wanted her, she would leave me. And if Michelle Pfeiffer entered our lives and wanted me, she knows I would go. We don't want to use commitment as a way to hold each other back or lessen life for each other."

This young couple has no idea of the horrible arrangement they have made with each other. What a self-deluding pretense at nobility! In the man's fantasy, Michelle Pfeiffer enters his life and then falls for him. For this improbable fantasy—and his wife's fantasy for Kevin Costner—they have refused to make a "for better or worse" lifetime commitment to each other. They make a huge sacrifice for the sake of keeping an escape clause, even if only in their minds.

The result for the man and his wife—and any couple who will not make their sex commitment exclusive, enduring through "better or worse"—is their sex lacks total abandonment and trust. With a potentially, or in actuality, unfaithful partner, sex must always have an element of self-protection. Uncommitted relationships lead to sexuality that can't afford the vulnerability of giving with abandon to each other. An unfaithful partner cannot be trusted not to abuse that kind of extreme vulnerability. In contrast, protection from betrayal means that a person can entrust his or her sexuality as a ministry.

A second sexual cost in uncommitted relationships is that very often the kind of sex being practiced by uncommitted partners is a sex marked by the passion of usage instead of a passion for the spouse. It's as if an interior voice says, "Well, you sure can't trust him or her, so just get what you can for now." Sex of this nature can never be satisfying, focused on each other, or fulfilling either physically or spiritually. It does not bring the relationship closer, but oddly distances each from the other. Sex with a user is like making love to a body while the "soul" is not at home. Sex outside of a committed framework is fallen and empty.

If there were a scale that measured the degree a couple enjoys spiritually intimate sexuality with one another, uncommitted sex would rank at the bottom. It can't compete with sex practiced according to God's ideal, which is sex experienced primarily as an enhancement of relationship, a way to nurture the exclusive bond of commitment and trust between a husband and wife. Exclusive mental and physical faithfulness with each other provides the environment for the ultimate and most satisfying sexual experiences.

Spiritual Intimacy Exercise 6
Five Words of Honor

> This exercise is simple, very tender, and in our experience, extremely profound. We assign you to use these five words to help you demonstrate honor and respect as you are relating sexually:
>
> "Thank you for loving me."
>
> Those five words can honor a spouse like few others. Say them to the one who brings you his or her soul, gives himself (herself) to you sexually, and cares for you in an expression of spiritual intimacy as none other can.

3. Respond Together in Sexual Expression

Commitment three is: "We will travel together in our sexual expression." This commitment means a husband and wife consider and respond to each other in their sexual expression. They choose to practice sex that is inclusive and mutually satisfying. They refuse to settle for sex that is primarily a solo performance with one partner unaware of the other's presence. They agree on methods, timing, places.

The spiritually intimate couple has a great advantage when it comes to discerning the difference between sex that is "abuser" sex—that is, sex that makes one person feel uncomfortable or filled with pain or shame by the other's sexual preferences—and sex that brings blessing into each other's life. This commitment promises to use that discernment in their sexual lives.

By committing to travel together sexually, a couple pursues each other's care and comfort in the ways they express their sexuality to and with each other. The sexual journey is a mutual experience with the goal of increasing their sensitivity to each other, not trampling one another in the pursuit of sexual passion. That means sexuality that is primarily one-way oriented—such as the between-the-knees self-satisfaction of our friend's husband—ignores the spouse and will always be less fulfilling (and respectful) than mutual expression.

4. Be Involved Wholly, with Soul and Body

Commitment four is: "We will be wholly involved in our sexual expression." If there ever was an appropriate place for passion in marriage, this is it. The commitment is to actively "be there." It means we will not hide our souls from each other behind masks of intolerance or passive disinterest. Passionate involvement with each other, the kind of lovemaking that reveals a person's innermost soul, is the kind of sex that only the most trusted, spiritually intimate couples can ever know.

A young couple came to us shortly after their honeymoon. Brenda was surprised by her lack of interest in his sexual advances. Stewart was disappointed, to say the least. During their courtship, Brenda had experienced all the symptoms of wanting him. But suddenly, in married life, he was so sexually present, so constant, so one-dimensional in his relating to her.

"What do we do?" Stewart lamented. "She doesn't like sex!"

As we searched for words to comfort and guide our young married friends, God reminded us of our own growth curve in sexual comfort with each other. We were in sexual first grade once ourselves.

"Realize that unless you want to miss it completely—and trust us, skipping the part of life that is sexual is a lot to miss!—you will need to put yourselves on a learning curve with each other. You can learn to enjoy sex more. And, additionally, if you ever learn to enjoy sex, it will be, by definition of your wedding vows, with each other. Are you really willing to miss that in life after such a short foray into physical intimacy?"

The two did want to try and were willing to put themselves on a learning curve that would let them understand each other's sexual needs and preferences and, over time, learn to appreciate the role of sex in their marriage. That was many years ago; today Brenda and Stewart are parents of several children. They have a sexual way of relating that is uniquely theirs and suited to their needs. They are happily married and doing well. A commitment to be involved includes a commitment to becoming increasingly comfortable with the vulnerable intimacy of sexual passion. It leads to soul-baring sex and increased satisfaction with your own and your spouse's sexuality.

5. Be Willing to Learn

Commitment five is: "We will continue to learn about our sexuality and our partner's sexual needs." Happily married older couples have recognized the importance of the sexual aspect of their marriage.

Years ago, as a young pastor's wife, I attended a course on human sexuality sponsored by a ministry organization. I found the experience fascinating and educational. Only women attended.

For six weeks we listened to speakers who encouraged us to view our sexuality as God's blessing. Every week we were given an assignment designed to encourage sexual attachment with our husbands. The next week the women would attend class and report on the homework assignment. The reports were amazingly discreet, considering the topic, delivered with humor and received with joy.

The older women amazed me. They always told the best, most genuine stories. With delightful candor and openness—much more so than the younger women—they laughed at themselves and their husbands. How wonderful to be interested learners about sexuality after all those years of marriage.

I left the course with a great life lesson: You're never too old to learn more about sex!

Young passions can make room through the years for increased knowledge and educated understanding. The commitment to be continual learners protects us against dullness in our sexual expressions with each other. Intentional and continual learning about your spouse's sexual needs will lead both of you to become better lovers through the years.

GOD'S BLESSING ON YOUR SEXUAL LIFE

God's blessing is on a married couple's sexual life. Perhaps the best question to ask is, how can we bring honor and respect to each other in the working out of our own unique sexual expressions? The answer is to use these five words during and after sexual relations: "Thank you for loving me." It is crucial; in fact, it forms Spiritual Intimacy Exercise 6 (see page 174).

"Thank you for loving me." That statement always conveys honor and respect to our lover. It will make your spouse feel appreciated and positive about the sexual experience and your presence in his or her life.

Give honor!

Show respect!

Say thank you to your partner for the gift of his or her sexuality in your life.

Recognize and honor the exclusive gift of each other's soul and body. Enjoy what God has blessed. After all, a Christian marriage, practicing the ministry of sexual care, using the blessing of physical love as a tool of God's expression to mate soul to soul is a rare wonder. Sexuality that is becoming increasingly spiritual in nature is a decided improvement to the norm.

A married love that includes sexual passion and romance is worth unpacking from its place of storage. Sexual expression is the intense marriage holiday that celebrates soulful love, that ministers tenderness in a world that couldn't care less. It pours life on each partner when the world has drained us dry. Indeed, in lighting dark sky with passion and wonder and awe, we couples can become more aware of God's goodness in our lives, even as we abandon ourselves into each other's care.

Afterimage

#1 Time alone with the Lord in Scripture and prayer.
*#2 Quality time communicating with my wife and giving
special attention to my two boys.*
*#3 Speaking words of affirmation and encouragement to an-
other person.*

(From Steve's January 15, 1980 journal entry listing
personal priorities to be accomplished daily)

11

Just
Don't
Ask
Me
to Pray!

We're often surprised at the things people say within earshot of others. Crowded together, waiting for a train in the depot, standing in a grocery checkout line, sitting in the bleachers of a football game, in between the "You don't say!" and the "C'mon, reallys?" are hidden life gems, rich in truth and irony. Recently we overheard this "jewel" between two women friends while we were standing in a crowded room together.

"Did you hear about Mary's funeral?" the elegant older woman asked in a stage whisper that could have filled any large auditorium.

"No, what happened?" responded the woman in red, her interest immediately piqued.

"Well, believe me, it was a first. Right in the middle of the service her ex, Harry, stood up and delivered a shocker, 'Mary was the love of my life. I know that may sound strange to some of you, but a divorce doesn't always end your feelings. I have always loved her—will always love her! We should never have divorced. I will miss her enormously.'"

"Really!" The lady in red was aghast. Her eyes widened to a state of extra alarm; her body seemed stiff with shock. She has provided her

friend, the storyteller, with the ultimately satisfying listener response
—total-body involvement. Obviously encouraged that the gossip mine
had been tested and found safe for further excavation, the older woman
continued.

"Oh, yes. And worst of all, his second wife was sitting right next to
him hearing that whole thing."

"Unbelievable. How shocking!" They threw in a few "Poor Marys"
and continued to tsk-tsk-tsk and tut-tut-tut until the gem's many
facets had been examined completely.

Poor Mary indeed. How sad to think that nothing short of death
can bring a loved one into an appreciative light. Death is the great un-
masker. What we could not see about someone while living becomes
clearly visible when he/she is gone from us. The real person emerges
more strongly into focus in our memories, and that which was not so
innately true about or worthy of him or her fades. Sometimes it takes
death to help expose what we were missing all the time.

As we debriefed that strange and sad funeral confession, I couldn't
help but wonder, *What would I most miss about Steve if I were to lose him?*
When I pass his essence through the possibility of death, one of the
things that comes strongly to the surface about Steve is the way he prays.

Through the years I have recognized a pattern in his prayers.
When he talks to God with me, I am comforted by his faith, strength-
ened by his hope, and encouraged to trust a little more, try a little
harder, and hang in there a little longer. When I am struggling, he
pours out his faith on me and covers me with his own spiritual stability. I try to do that for him as well.

THE SPIRITUAL INTIMACY OF PRAYER IN MARRIAGE

Letting God In

Struggling at times in marriage is common and should be expected. Whenever one or both spouses are going through difficult times,
they can wait in God's presence and together seek His wisdom and
guidance. When you pray as a couple, you "let God in." During those
joint times of prayerful seeking, God seems the closest, His comforting
presence somehow closing the gaps in the relationship. God's resources seem personally attainable, and faith is alive with possibilities
surpassing what can only be hinted at by the God defined in some distant theological tenet. As you pray together, life seems the safest. The
intimate sharing and the deep connecting of prayer together is like the

cream of a marriage. In prayer we can have intimate knowledge of the shape of one another's souls.

If tomorrow I woke up to a new chapter in my life and found that our marriage was over, that my husband had gone home to God, I would miss many things. Surely I would miss the ease of our companionship built up through the years. I would miss my sexual partner and ache for our children's loss of the best father in the world. I would miss Steve's joy, his high-energy engagement with life, his provision, and his care. But if I lost him to death, I would most miss the comfort of our spiritual intimacy—our prayer life together, the tender care expressed in his words about me and God, his articulated faith, his shared love of God.

The Difficulty of Praying Together

The spiritual intimacy of prayer is a powerful connecting, comforting, healing medicine, and yet it seems to be so underrated by Christian couples today. Indeed, one of the most difficult areas of spiritual intimacy for couples is praying together. Reportedly, marriage seminars that have been proceeding at full speed through communication issues, sexuality issues, and gender issues will come to an abrupt stop if couples are asked to turn to each other and pray together. One marriage seminar leader even considered taking the prayer segment out of his Christian marriage seminar because, asking couples to respond on-the-spot was like running into a brick wall of hesitancy and resistance.

Why is that? we wonder. We recognize that a high percentage of couples attending a seminar to receive help in their marriage likely already have a number of preexisting issues and that the hesitancy to pray together may reflect the miner's bird effect: Spiritual intimacy is just too uncomfortable and is sounding an alarm about the relationship's health. Perhaps it is reasonable that praying together, under those circumstances, will not be well received.

Still, we were curious. Are feelings of discomfort with shared prayer more representative of "troubled" Christian marriages, or were the resisting responses of couples attending marriage seminars more the "norm" than some of us in Christian leadership realize? Throughout the year of writing this book, Valerie and I conducted our own informal survey, making it a point to ask various couples about their prayer lives together. Their responses verified that resistance to a shared life of prayer extends to healthy Christian marriages. There seems to be an existing gap between the "ideal" of Christian husbands and wives praying together and the reality.

TALES FROM THE FRONT

What follows—from some very well marriages, marriages without resistance to spiritual intimacy because of obvious preexisting problems—are some of the reasons for this gap between the ideal and the actual. Listen to what these four spouses say:

"Oh, praying together would never work at our house. David is so self-conscious about finding the right words for prayer. Our church background is more formal and liturgical, and we have just never learned comfortable, informal, spontaneous praying. He'd die if I asked him to pray out loud with me!"

"We've tried to pray together, but we had to give it up. It became such an intense production between the two of us. We felt we had to keep up with each other's prayer abilities, and so we struggled remembering that God was the One we were speaking to. It's just easier to pray on our own."

"My husband is more intense and driven than I am. I've always felt uncomfortable praying with him. It's like I was the spiritual pygmy and he was the spiritual giant. We were too lopsided spiritually to make it work."

"We simply avoid the traditional spiritual disciplines. Our problem is a lack of motivation. We've never gotten much out of it. It feels awkward, and to be honest, somewhat pointless. It seems to be another one of those 'should' areas like flossing your teeth, regular medical checkups, or daily exercise that, of course, would be nice, but you can get through the day without it."

At one stage or another in our marriage, we could relate to almost all of the ways those couples told us they avoided prayer.

FOUR FUNDAMENTAL SPIRITUAL DISCIPLINES

The final speaker mentioned prayer as being among the traditional spiritual disciplines. We want to address more than prayer in this chapter, for many couples who avoid prayer also avoid other spiritual disciplines. We have found that avoiding the traditional disciplines is missing an opportunity to come closer to God and to each other.

Valerie and I also have occasional spells where we feel unmotivated or undisciplined. Yet, we always return to the classics: prayer, Scripture, worship, and journaling. We know they are valuable. They've proven so in our lives over the long term and historically in the lives of others as well.

Without question, we also know that we really can't get through tomorrow—at least get through tomorrow well—without them. And while we understand that methodology is basically a means to integrated spirituality and that spiritual disciplines are a means to an end, the classic Christian disciplines of shared prayer, Scripture reading, worship, and journaling hold tremendous creative resources for spiritual growth and oneness in a couple's life.

So, from a couple who are true believers in the benefits of the disciplines of spiritual intimacy in marriage, even though we sometimes struggle to maintain them, here are some insights that might motivate others to keep trying.

A DEVELOPED TASTE

The classic Christian disciplines, like most finer things in life, seem to be a developed taste. This is especially true with prayer.

Think, for instance, how musical tastes develop over a lifetime. A child listening to his first Beethoven symphony will not be as appreciative a listener as a person who has spent decades developing his or her musical tastes. A child's ear can be overwhelmed by a symphony, and when exposed to it, may be inclined to return to simpler musical forms. That's why "Barney" music, while boring to adult ears, is the choice of kids. In contrast, a trained musical ear hears what others can't: the recapitulation of musical themes resounding in varying textures throughout the instrumental sections of the orchestra, the harmonic and rhythmic counterthemes, the pinching whine of a solo oboe, or the delicate cry of the violins. Music connoisseurs get more out of music than other people do.

Developing a Taste for Prayer

Prayer also is a developed taste. It ranges from a simple cry for "Help!" to the deepest, most eloquently articulated searching for God. And while there is absolutely nothing wrong with a childlike prayer for help, it may be somewhat simple-souled in light of the vast possibilities of God-connectedness available in prayer. In other words, there is a vast ocean of connectedness to God and each other when we are willing to move off the shore of prayers called "Help!" and explore what lies beyond.

The seasoned pray-er experiences prayer through a developed soul. What is an awkward silence where words will not come for some, is for a seasoned pray-er an exquisite silence, a moment when God can reveal Himself to a word-quieted soul.

A seasoned pray-er experiences incredible fulfillment in prayer. But getting to that level, for most of us, requires a learning curve, and as in any other area requiring discipline to learn—a musical instrument, computers, a foreign language—the learning curve can be tedious. We are all demotivated with things that produce boredom in our lives. When we are passive and uninvolved, it is unrealistic to expect God somehow to make prayer miraculously interesting. To develop a taste for prayer, to sense fulfillment with the discipline, will require the pursuit of it like any other interest in life. Collectors of train sets, blue willow china, and antique tools all know where to chase them down. Motivation is defined by passion. And passion is defined by the return on the investment.

With prayer, in order to be motivated, a person must hang in there long enough to begin to experience some return on the investment. The husband returning from a Promise Keepers' event with a charge to become the spiritual leader in his home by initiating some basic spiritual disciplines may be tempted to give it up after a few seemingly fruitless tries. He needs assurance that there is enough return on the investment of his efforts. He needs to keep at it until comfort and ease and enjoyment kick in.

The return on the investment of prayer together as a couple is enormous. Prayer can provide the basis for spiritual intimacy that helps a couple drive their imperfect marriage machine, regardless of its "mechanical malfunctions." Prayer is the tool for the deepest soulful connecting between a husband and wife and the God they love. God's presence bridges whatever gaps a couple experience together and resources the grace of heaven that can move them from a marriage of toleration into a marriage that is on its way to success—a marriage that is becoming as good as it can be.

With shared prayer, one of the finer of the finest things in life, a marriage experiences a quality of relating beyond human experience. Praying together invites God in, and with Him comes the too-good-to-be-true relational miracle, the hint of hope, the touch of wonder, the new, clear perspective. With time and practice, the couple will sense

God's closeness, regard each other as sweet, and feel that the world of-fers a less attractive claim on their lives.

What couple would not want what prayer can do for their marriage?

The classic spiritual discipline of prayer can be increasingly en-joyed and appreciated for Christian couples on the spiritual learning curve. The secret is to keep trying.

> According to Jesus, by far the most important thing about prayer is to keep at it. . . . Be importunate Jesus says—not, one assumes, because you have to beat a path to God's door before he'll open it, but because until you beat the path maybe there's no way of getting to *your* door. "Ravish my heart," John Donne wrote. But God will not usually ravish. He will only court.[1]

Developing a Taste for the Other Spiritual Disciplines

Three other classic disciplines of Bible reading, worship, and keeping a spiritual journal also are an acquired taste. They don't come easily; much can distract us from practicing them with our spouse. The final spiritual intimacy exercise we're including, "Developing a Taste for the Classics," offers some ideas for developing discipline in each of these spiritual practices. Among our suggestions are to read through a one-year Bible, purchase and use a hymnal, and read one or more devotional books. Like the discipline of prayer, the practices of Scripture reading, worship, and journaling come easier with practice. You must take time to have time.

We recommend two steps to help develop a regular, ongoing time with these disciplines: (1) set a time to connect spiritually and (2) learn to use downtime to connect. First, setting a specific time (weekly works well for us) for spiritual learning has major benefits. A "spiritual date" works for some couples because it provides an acceptable way to begin acclimating to a deeper level of conversation with each other. Bring your one-year Bible, your journals, your notes, whatever, to this meeting. Simply share what you've been reading or learning. This kind of integration is so healthy. Even though you did not initially "dig out" your insights together, it still builds toward spiritual intimacy as you take the time to share your thoughts.

Second, downtime from busy schedules offers good opportunities to connect spiritually. Taking a trip, even a short one? Why not spend a portion of the time in the car worshiping together? Drive and pray (with your eyes open), together sing some worship songs with a cassette tape or CD, talk about your individual spiritual learning curves, or be vulnerable about your anxieties and pressures. Practice having spiritual conversations. Capture some of this downtime to enjoy God and connect together with Him.

THE GOAL: INTIMACY WITH GOD

Going Beyond Methods and Techniques

There is a tension in the practice of the classic spiritual disciplines. What place or value should they hold in a couple's shared life? How necessary are they to spiritual growth? As the final person in "Tales from the Front" noted, sometimes practicing the disciplines "feels awkward, and . . . somewhat pointless."

Doug Rumford writes in *Soul Shaping: Taking Care of Your Spiritual Life,*

> As we explore the area of spiritual disciplines, we should keep in mind that spiritual vitality resists the mechanical use of methods and techniques. As with any relationship, love and respect—not manipulation—guide the deepening life. *Spiritual vitality grows out of our relationship with the Lord Jesus.*
>
> But spiritual exercise can help put us in a place where we are more receptive to God's grace and goodness. Even though the process of spiritual growth is in many ways mysterious, *there are steps we can take* to develop spiritual sensitivity, . . . to align our disoriented and dissatisfied lives with God's purposes. *There are ways* in which we can put ourselves in touch with God's power.[2]

Jan Johnson expresses well the need for those using spiritual disciplines to keep the ultimate goal in mind: "I had complicated the spiritual life with my notebook and checklists and invented my own version of 'spiritual correctness.' In truth I needed only one thing—God. I didn't need a great quiet time, I needed a God-centered lifetime. I saw that my responsibility as a Christian was to seek God's company, not to seek spiritual maturity."[3]

Living a spiritually correct life, placing a check mark on the spiritual to-do list, developing a system for acquiring spiritual knowledge —how far short these approaches to Scripture and prayer fall from the ideal of connectedness to God. The end result of a spiritually-disciplined life is not becoming puffed up with accomplishment and pride for being on the spiritual achievement fast track. Rather, the spiritual disciplines are properly functioning in our lives when there is an increased awareness of our utter dependence on God, when we experience a growing sense of His great lavish love for ourselves and all humankind. Effective spiritual disciplines will lead us to a growing hunger for more that is of God. The spiritual disciplines are merely aids that can enable us to run to God in total abandonment of soul.

But how necessary are the shared spiritual disciplines between a husband and wife? Can't a couple grow through Christian radio, listening to sermons and Christian music, and reading Christian literature? With everything that is available today, does a couple actually need to have a traditional, shared devotional life in order to be spiritually connected?

Going Beyond What We Think

We believe the classic spiritual disciplines are essential to a couple's spiritual growth, as vital to spiritual growth in marriage as vacuums, dust rags, and cleansing agents are to a clean home. Just as you cannot think your way into a clean home—clearing the fridge of leftovers, washing the dishes, and wiping the countertops require actual work—so spiritual growth is not just about "how we think." Soul work needs the tools of prayer, Scripture, worship, and journaling to achieve its ultimate goal—a deepening spiritual connectedness to God and to each other. To get to application and integration a couple needs to use the tools of spiritual growth.

God wants a relationship with you. A secondhand relationship with you through your pastor, or the words of a Christian songwriter, or another person's spiritual processing is not intimate enough for God. He wants your heart. The classic spiritual disciplines deliver you up to God in a personal way that secondhand growth can never accomplish.

Meeting the Firsthand, Accessible God

The times when God reveals Himself to us through the spiritual disciplines—when He "jumps off the page" of a Scripture passage or when a prayer-quieted heart hears an inner voice of spiritual truth and recognizes it as such—are the high-water marks, the soul's reference points in the spiritual afterimages of our lives. One of the core messages of Scripture is that every believing man, woman, and child has direct access to God. He is personal, appropriate, and profoundly connecting. He is firsthand accessible to each of us.

Shortly after Valerie became pregnant with Brendan, her father was struck with encephalitis. Until his death four and a half years later, his body lived on, an empty shell where an exceptional mind and a spiritually sensitive soul had once resided. Valerie, like the rest of the family, was devastated. Brokenhearted. And broken-souled.

In time, we knew his situation was not only desperate, but hopeless. Apart from a miracle, faith seemed pointless. Valerie fell into what I can only describe as a "spiritual depression" which became the background for an afterimage, a reference point, that happened while she was reading Scripture. That Scripture, like a bottle floating on a wind-tossed sea, contained a message of comfort and deliverance. With a long look back, she understood that the crisis had floated her misbeliefs to the surface of the water like the pieces of a boat that had crashed and capsized.

Where is God's care? she had wondered over and over. *Why doesn't He answer our prayers? What good is faith if nothing ever changes?* There in the wreckage, as she struggled to keep her head of faith above the waves, bobbed debris of confusion and sharp shards of anger with God.

Valerie's rescue came during one reading of Scripture. As she explains, "I was lost and drowning in deep unresolvable grief. As my father's crisis wore on, my Bible went increasingly unread, but for some reason, without expecting much, I was dutifully reading it one day and came to these words: 'Listen, O daughter, consider and give ear: forget your people and your father's house. . . . Your sons will take the place of your fathers; you will make them princes throughout the land'" (Psalm 45:10, 16).

What is this? I wondered. *A specific message in a bottle floating on my sea of ruin? What does it mean?*

"I knew I would never forget my father or my father's house, but I caught the wave of truth in those words. Concerning my father, I realized, that if he could have said anything to me personally during those days of his muteness and absenteeism, it would have been something like, 'Valerie, do not let this ruin your life. You have a husband. You have a child. Trust me to God.'

"Could it be that God, my heavenly Father, was mirroring what I knew my earthly father would have wanted for me: encouragement to move beyond grief, beyond heartbreak, to new life, new beginnings, and a new understanding of family?"

That's what Valerie concluded. And after many years, those words from Scripture make even more sense: "Two grown sons later, I recognize the wisdom of those words, their amazing specificity, their deep kindness, their call to hope and faith and trust."

Who says God is at a distance? Not us. There are too many high-water marks in our lives, too many personalizations of Scripture, too many quiet, still voices of truth in prayer for us to ever think of God as removed, uninvolved, and disconnected.

That is why a firsthand, personalized faith is so important. The spiritual disciplines of prayer, Bible study, worship, and journaling are the tools that "dig out" our personal relationship, our individualized connecting points to God. We may recognize truth when we hear it in a song, in a message, in a spoken testimony, but until it is "our" truth it will not have the same impact. It will not be as motivational or as convincing of the personal return on spiritual investment.

THE CHALLENGE: DOING IT TOGETHER

"But it's so hard to practice spiritual disciplines together," you may say. We agree. Togetherness in the classic spiritual disciplines takes some understanding of each other's spiritual processing.

Author and pastor Walter Wangerin describes his own hesitancy at entering into spiritual intimacy with his wife:

> Once, early in our marriage, Thanne asked that we pray aloud together. I hesitated. Today I confess that the idea caused me discomfort—something a bit too intimate to be done in front of another human being, even one's spouse. I was attending seminary, preparing for ministry; but I liked things more formal, less personal. I hesitated then for weeks and months.
>
> But there came a day when I committed some sin against Thanne. She said, "We have to pray aloud together. We have to."
>
> I said, "I'll start."
>
> Of course I would start. I was studying for the ministry. I was the husband. It was my duty. Besides I was a wizard at words.
>
> So I prayed in heavy cadences, like a hymnal, grandiloquent and measured and gassy with abstractions. When I was done I congratulated myself on having accomplished a difficult thing after all.
>
> But then the voice of my wife arose in the darkness. In simple language she was talking to God. Just talking. Her tone was so soft, it seemed that they were alone together, while I was allowed to listen, like an eavesdropper.
>
> Her humility humbled me. There was no grandeur left in my soul.
>
> And then, as she was speaking to God, she named my name! Not to me, but to God she murmured "Wally" with such love and gentleness that I began to cry. In the plain precincts of her prayer Thanne's love became a holy thing. It brought the breathing Spirit of God down upon my silly soul and I cried.[4]

Spiritual Intimacy Exercise 7
Developing a Taste for the Classics

The spiritual disciplines of prayer, reading Scripture, worship, and journaling are the classic ways of accessing God into our lives. When shared by a husband and wife, they invite God into a marriage. Here are six ways you can develop your taste for these classic disciplines:

1. Begin using a one-year Bible. A one-year Bible divides Scripture into 365 daily portions. The length of each daily passage is not too long. You can use these Bibles like workbooks: highlight significant passages, write in the margins, date prayer requests and answers to prayer in the margins. An unexpected return on this investment of time is that the next year when you return to that reading, there is a record, a sketchy journaling of where you were spiritually the previous year.

2. Maintain a journal. Many people are surprised at their own insights, depth, and spirituality when they begin to put their thoughts down on paper. Until it is in black and white, your insights are only floating through your mind—and usually out of your mind. In a journal you can keep anything that is worthy of preservation: notes from sermons, quotes from magazines, newspaper clippings, or book passages, even interesting conversations you've had. A journal is a preserver of life's most meaningful moments and responses to those moments. Later, when you reread the entries about God, His world, and your responses to it, you can recall a great thought, an excellent word usage, a fresh or creative idea.

3. Obtain a hymnal and a Christian songbook. While we're taking time to read Scripture, we find it's also a good time occasionally to read or sing through some spiritual songs and worship God either alone or together. The words are rich in experience and theology.

Scripture songs are familiar and singable. Just pick one, lift up your heart to God, and sing with abandoned soul. Music loosens the inhibited soul, and it is a great emotional connector to a listening God.

4. Pick up a devotional book—or two or three. There are so many choices in devotional readings. Most are also divided into daily readings. We enjoy using these short devotionals together and will vary our readings with different authors quite a bit. Remember, the goal is not just to check this off the to-do list, but to use the material as stimuli for processing together. Discuss it, sharing observations. Ask such questions as, "What do you hear? How does this apply in our lives?"

5. Tell each other about specific incidents when you have sensed God's involvement in your life. Spouses usually tell Christian friends about God's working in their lives—how He had helped them accomplish a difficult task or surprised them with a solution from "out of the blue"— before they tell their spouse. Indeed, often the husband or wife is the last one to hear such things. Unless couples are intentional about sharing spiritually, the normal tendency is to bypass talking with each other on this level.

6. Pick a time of the day to pray for each other. We know a couple who sets aside a few minutes every day at 2:00 in the afternoon to pray for each other. They know that no matter what else is happening in their lives, no matter how many miles are separating them, the other will be lifting them up to God for His protection and care. We like this idea, although we recognize a specific, set-aside time may not work with every couple's schedule. But it is still a great connector to agree together to pray for each other during the day. Make the prayers specific by asking your spouse questions like: "What's on your plate today? How can I best pray for you to make it through the day? What pressures do you feel most keenly at the moment?" Such questions will help you to connect spiritually,

with the implied promise that you will remember each other during the day while absent from each other.

One final suggestion deserves special consideration. Pray Scripture on behalf of your spouse. Sincere prayers using Scripture can bring comfort and inspiration to your mate. Such prayers should be laced with grace, love, protection, and care. Sometimes I go directly to the Bible and literally pray Scripture over Valerie, inserting her name right into the passage.

Many different passages can be used. They can enhance your prayer lives for each other tremendously! You can also do this together. Here's an example from Psalm 63:

"O God, you are [our] God, earnestly [Valerie and I] seek you; [our souls] thirst for you, [our bodies] long for you, in a dry and weary land where there is no water. [We] have seen you in the sanctuary and beheld your power and your glory. Because your love is better than life, [Valerie's and my] lips will glorify you. [We] will praise you as long as [we] live, and in your name [we] will lift up [our] hands . . ."

Hearing a spouse pray your name right into God's Word is both uplifting and a good reminder of God's involvement in your life.

✳   ✳   ✳

What husband and wife have the same spiritual style? Probably few come at spirituality in the same way, with the same expectations, and with the same comfort levels. And that diversity—of our perspectives and approach to God—much like our diversity in personalities, passions, and gifts, is a key reason we need to practice the disciplines *together,* as husbands and wives. It's worth the effort to include your spouse.

As you form spiritually, growing together gives the two of you great advantage. We learned this during our years working in Christian radio. For twelve years, Steve served as broadcast cohost, speaker, and associate director of *The Chapel of the Air,* and for ten years Valerie produced the daily fifteen-minute nationally syndicated program. During most weeks a part of our responsibilities was to prepare one or two radio broadcasts together. Publicly, we called this presentation format "dialoging." But privately we often called it something else.

This was not an easy exercise. At best it was difficult. Sometimes painfully difficult. The biggest challenge was bringing our opposite creative processes into the mix. Valerie, with her set-off-from-shore-and-let's-just-see-where-the-boat-takes-us preferred style, up against my outlines, linear logic, and organized end-result-in-mind approach.

We bantered. Our discussions would intensify. Our goal was to achieve the "door open" policy so we could prepare together without arguing or becoming frustrated with each other. We rarely achieved our goal. A typical morning working through a Scripture passage together (behind closed doors) often went something like this:

"What are you trying to say, Valerie? How can you possibly get that interpretation out of this passage? It's not central. It's quirky."

"Oh, loosen up. There is more than one correct way to interpret things spiritually."

"Yes, I agree, but at the moment we're getting nowhere. We have a broadcast to record in one hour, and we aren't even close to being ready!"

"Well, then, why don't you listen to me so we can get something accomplished here?"

"Because we have to be theologically accurate and we need to have a point!"

Not that Valerie was ever opposed to having a point, but how we got there mattered immensely to her.

Sometimes our struggle was all about power. Each of us wanted the final word about direction and interpretation. Our creative styles and how differently each of us processed content were enormous issues for us. As the broadcast deadline loomed nearer, we would become increasingly edgy with each other. But the clock was ticking, so we would have to come to some form of agreement.

As the years went by, we became much more accomplished at preparing broadcasts, but during those times of struggle it did not feel like we were connecting. It rarely felt intimate. It felt, if anything, more off-putting.

Unaware to us initially, all those years of hammering out our different spiritual styles and creative processes helped in that our spiritual formation was occurring together. The separate sheets of parchment were fusing. We had been on a learning curve with each other's souls and saw them naked. We were frustrated, yes, but also bare-hearted and totally open to each other, to examination and process.

We were forming spiritually with each other. We knew the shape of each other's souls; we understood each other's most intimate spiritual processing and conception of God.

That is why it is so important—regardless of a couple's dissimilar styles, expectations, or differing facility—to work through the spiritual disciplines together as a couple. There is no better way to "know" each other than through the intimate, occasionally difficult process of sharing and interpreting Scripture together, praising God together, seeking Him together, and learning to enjoy Him together. The times of discussing Scripture and spiritual matters may point out your differences, may lead to disagreement, and even, on occasion, to tension. But they allow you to understand each other better as you deal with deeper issues of life and spirit. And they give you personal experiences together —experiences that are common to you two alone—that will deepen your spiritual relationship.

Looking back, preparing radio broadcasts hammered out behind closed doors was incredibly good for our spiritual formation. And although we've described our struggle in this area, we strongly believe that the return on the investment in terms of spiritual intimacy is worth whatever relational roadblocks appear as a couple pursues the spiritual disciplines together.

SOME PRACTICAL POINTERS

As your spouse and you begin to practice the spiritual disciplines, consider these practical pointers. First, start simple. Your spouse initially may show resistance. Although it's preferable to be able to share this growth area together, you still can begin alone. Second, practice the two time suggestions mentioned earlier in this chapter: (1) set a time to connect spiritually and (2) learn to use downtime to connect. The time should be regular (probably one or more times each week), but need not be limited to those set times. Look for other times when you both can connect for spiritual learning, such as during a short trip together in the car.

Third, process spiritual ideas and applications with your spouse whenever possible. Whether you had a spiritual conversation with your child, heard a radio commentary with a spiritual implication, or just came back from an inspiring worship service, make time to share with your spouse as soon as possible.

Many opportunities for connecting spiritually wife to husband (and vice versa) are lost because we forget or let other activities clutter our day. Tell your mate what you heard as soon as possible, both to share your enthusiasm and to process the idea, clarifying it with your partner.

This is especially helpful after a church service. During the drive home, instead of heading off into the afternoon—deciding where to eat, what to do with the free time, how to get the kids to their activities—spend the drive or time over lunch processing what church was about. Share with each other what you heard God saying to you during some part of the service. Maybe the music ministered to you in a particular way, or the smile of an usher or greeter made you feel like you belonged, or an encouraging comment someone gave you, or the words from a Scripture passage, or the content of the message. This kind of conversation will go a long way in making that which is spiritual a normal, healthy part of family life.

The hour after church is probably the greatest unmined hour for spiritual learning, continued sensitivity, and connectedness to God in the life of most families. As much as possible, develop the good spiritual habit of editing all intruders and demands on that time and, instead, *respond* to that hour and *share* it with each other.

PRAYERS USING SCRIPTURE

The final suggestion for developing a taste for the classic disciplines (see Spiritual Intimacy Exercise 7) was to pray Scripture: Pray Bible verses aloud on behalf of and in the presence of your spouse. Concerning such prayers, we want to give a caution. The prayers have tremendous potential to affirm your spouse spiritually, but they also can be misused. Be wary of having a prayer agenda, one that presumes to know where your spouse *should be* spiritually. Yes, you may pray with your spouse that he or she will come to experience in a fuller way the love of God. But some prayer agendas carry such a heavy load of "holy" expectation of change for the other that we fear a lack of grace and acceptance lying behind such prayers. We would not appreciate such an agenda prayed over us. For example:

"Dear God, help my husband to see the error of his ways, the mismanagement of his time, his inability to establish priorities, his self-centeredness. He's just too laid back, Lord; I can hardly stand it sometimes. Make him a man of conviction, and help him to finally take some personal responsibility for his obvious shortcomings." Or

"Oh, Lord, make my wife a woman of God with enthusiasm for her role as a homemaker and the one responsible for the kids. . . . I mean, she's a kept woman and has it so good and doesn't even realize it! And, oh yes, give her some joy too . . . and patience. Lord, you've probably noticed how lacking she is in these areas. I can hardly handle it when she gets so down and negative about life . . ."

Instead, create prayers from Scripture focusing on passages of hope. As you pray Scripture on behalf of your mate, you can insert his or her name right into the passage. Take, for example, the text from Hebrews 4:14–16, in which I've inserted my wife's name:

"Therefore, since [Valerie has] a great high priest who has gone through the heavens, Jesus the Son of God, let [her] hold firmly to the faith [she] profess[es]. For [Valerie does] not have a high priest who is unable to sympathize with [her] weaknesses, but [she has] one who has been tempted in every way, just as [she is]—yet was without sin. Let [Valerie] then approach the throne of grace with confidence, so that [she] may receive mercy and find grace to help [her] in [her] time of need."

Or try this same approach with the Twenty-third Psalm. See how it feels or fits. Many different passages used like this can enhance your prayer lives for each other tremendously!

It is a wonder to hear a spouse pray your name right into God's Word. It's such a comfort for a wife or husband to know that their spouse's love is wrapped in prayer around his or her life.

TO KNOW AND BE KNOWN

Someone once said that the greatest need of human beings is to know and be known. We suppose that means more than just knowing how someone drinks coffee or which side of the bed is preferred. For husbands and wives we think it means knowing each other's souls.

I know my husband's soul. I have heard his heart cry out for me and cover me with spiritual protection and soulful care. He knows the shape of my soul as no one else ever will. Through prayer, Scripture, and shared spiritual intimacy we have entered into each other's souls and found that God is near.

That is our prayer for you as well. In practicing these spiritual disciplines with your spouse, together you can better know each other and your God. Come to God together, so that, in that sweet place where your hearts join to His, you will experience the fulfillment of your deepest longings, to know and be known.

Afterimage

"For this God is our God for ever and ever; he will be our guide even to the end."

(Text to Psalm 48:14—the Scripture reference that is engraved in both Steve's and Valerie's wedding bands exchanged on June 20, 1970)

12

Leaving the Lights On

*L*ast summer during a break from graduate school, our older son, Brendan, worked as a counselor in a behavioral hospital for children and teenagers. The patients' conditions varied: children with autism who required one-on-one care to prevent them from damaging themselves; some who have no control over their impulses; children and teens who fought all authority; many who needed drugs to treat their compulsiveness; still others who are broken children of abuse; adolescent sex offenders whose only other alternative would be prison. On and on went the sad stories.

Most of the time Brendan never had to wonder what anyone was thinking. Everyone said exactly what was on his mind, as if the interior editor never showed up.

One Sunday Brendan attended the hospital chapel service. A visitor shared her spiritual journey—complete with crystals and shaman-like prayers to the Great Spirit. It was too much for one of the patients. She interrupted the woman's message and challenged the visitor with her own beliefs—straight from some right-wing, rifle-toting cult. Brendan's head was swimming. He thought maybe he, a Christian college graduate, should say something. But before he had a chance, one of the younger girls stood up, dramatically threw her arms into the air, stretched her head to heaven, and with charming sincerity shouted, "God help us!"

Her unedited response delighted Brendan. It was his thought exactly.

THE SILENT CRY: "GOD HELP US"

"God help us" is the silent cry of all our hearts—a prayer expressing equal measures of despair and hope. Most of us, if we are honest, will thrust our arms at heaven, admit our insufficiency, throw ourselves on God's mercy, and ask for His intervention. When either of us does so, God seems at times to respond in silence to our pleas. But also it seems, especially as we review the afterimages of our life, that miraculously, in ways we could never predict, sometimes He obviously *does* reach out to us and helps us through.

"God help us." It is a good prayer.

The Married Lonely

"God help us" seems an especially appropriate prayer for the married lonely, the spiritually isolated, those whose spouses are unmotivated, disengaged, or opposed to spiritual closeness. It was the lonely heart cry of King David, a man with spiritual ardor and soulful abandonment, who endured his wife Michal's disdain and rejection of his worship. Like many who are reading this book, David no doubt was a lonely spiritual man, a solo traveler, an unmatched heart.

Perhaps you find yourself married to a withholder. Your heart cries out, "Love me. Come to God with me." But it is in vain. Maybe you have heard and responded to the inner voice that tells you "You were made to be loved," and have found God's love to be sufficient. Yet a part of you is also saddened. To travel through life without a real partner seems more cruel than you can sometimes bear. And you are right. To withhold anything a spouse needs seems merciless, if not sinful. And among the cruelest withholdings, right alongside withholding of love or withholding of sex, has to be withholding spiritual intimacy from a mate.

Maybe you understand this kind of loneliness, the aching neediness of soul that yearns to meld with your spouse in joyful prayer, thanksgiving, and spiritual comforts of the most exquisite kinds. Perhaps you are like that sculpted pair we described in the introduction.

God is remolding you, but your partner still leans away, hard as metal, uncomfortable and shunning anything spiritual.

A Cry of Hope . . . and Despair

"God help us" is the cry of the married lonely—a cry of hope. But if it expresses hope, it also expresses despair. That same heart can't help but wonder, *Will God hear? Will He work in my spouse's heart?*

There is always hope when it comes to what God might do. And, at any rate, it seems that we are so programmed for spiritual intimacy —as if that longing were a part of our genetic structure—that we can never give up hoping for it in our marriage, even if it seems an impossible possibility. It is too beautiful not to be desired, too right to ignore.

"God help us." We can't help but utter such a prayer for our less-than-they-should-be marriages.

THE MOST PRECIOUS GIFT

So, what can we do in a marriage where spiritual intimacy is hoped for but not forthcoming? Psychiatrist Gerald May suggests one attitude that might surprise you:

> We have this idea that everyone should be . . . totally whole, totally together spiritually, and totally fulfilled. In reality, our lack of fulfillment is the most precious gift we have. It is the source of our passion, our creativity, our search for God. All the best in life comes out of *our human yearning—our not being satisfied.* Certainly Scripture and religious tradition point out that we are not to be satisfied. We are meant to go on . . . seeking. Paul tells the Greeks in Athens that God created us to seek him.[1]

Two Choices

We can choose how this unrequited longing for human connectedness will play out in our lives. We can resent; we can resist the pain and insist that God deliver us. We can even give up on God. That is one set of choices—to turn the outrage and frustration towards God. We can view Him as the ultimate withholder, the One responsible for our partner's distance. But even if our marriage never fulfills or satisfies us, anybody with any spiritual insight understands that it would be further sadness to turn away from *His* comfort and love.

The other choice is to *allow the pain to induce spiritual growth.* Will we submit to this pain, accept it for the time being, and move closer to God and let Him form us to His heart?

The choice we make is crucial for two reasons. It has an enormous impact on our own life satisfaction, but it also has a potential impact on a spiritually distant spouse. The choice to turn on God and abandon hope turns off the light. Now two are in darkness. The choice to mold to God's love not only matures us spiritually, but leaves the light on for a spouse lost in the dark.

A Light of Hope

Our pastor gave the following illustration in a sermon recently: A man and his wife lived on a cliff overlooking the ocean. The man was a passionate seaman. One day, while he was sailing, a storm blew in suddenly. The sky darkened and the combination of fierce piercing rain and rolling waves threatened to swamp his struggling craft. Although he was not far from his home, he could see nothing in the darkness and soon lost his bearings entirely. He lost his sense of place and knew that without a visual anchor he could easily be dashed to pieces on the undetectable rocky coastline.

His wife sensed his danger. Desperately she lit every lamp in their home. *Perhaps this is foolish,* she thought. *He may have already drowned; or maybe he's too far from home to see the light. Is this helping him at all?* Despite her anxious thoughts, she kept the lamps lit through the long, uncertain night.

Her husband was just under the cliffs by their home and through the storm could faintly see their lit-up home. And although he could not sail his boat through the storm, her lights gave him his bearings. He no longer needed to see the rocks to know where they were in relationship to their home—they were near him, and he must steer the boat away. He worked all night to maneuver away from those rocks.

His was a desperate struggle to survive; yet he felt less alone and less afraid knowing that she was up waiting and praying for him. He exhausted himself for the sake of her hope and her lights. When the night passed and with the first rays of morning light, the storm passed, and he returned home to his relieved wife.

His wife's lights had given him his bearings and hope during the dark night of his struggle. Without her lighting the lamps in their home, he would have died on the rocks directly beneath where they lived.

In an uneven marriage of spiritually disconnected partners, it's important for the grounded one to leave the lights on for the one who is struggling. Like the seaman's wife, we only know our spouse is lost; we have no idea how close to "Home"—heaven—he or she may actually be. No one can ever adequately assess another person's spiritual condition. Apparent disinterest or opposition to a spiritual agenda may actually hide a heart that is softening and seeking. A spouse's unwavering spiritual light could be the method God uses in a marriage to give hope, spiritual bearings, and comfort to the one who is lost, but on the way "Home."

HOW SPIRITUAL LIGHTS CAN SHOW THE WAY

Through Divorce

Several years ago an older Christian woman we will call Helen left the lights on for her husband. He left her after many years of marriage, after their children were gone. He also left the church. No one could change his mind. Not his children, his pastor, his wife, their friends. All pleas to come to his senses fell on deaf ears. For a year or two he lived with a younger woman, eventually divorcing his wife to marry his new love. Helen was devastated emotionally during this period that spanned several years. Worst of all, she could not stop loving her husband, to disconnect and "move on with her life" as her friends counseled her. They had been married too long for a divorce paper to ever change how Helen felt about this man.

When Helen told Steve and me this story, we anticipated that she would share with us how the Lord had healed her heart and helped her move on with her life. Instead the older woman's story concluded with a surprise: "Two years ago he left his younger wife, came back home, and we were remarried. We have never been so happy!"

Between the lines of that woman's story is another whole book about forgiveness, but for now, let's recognize Helen's story as a marvelous example of what God may do when the stronger spiritual partner refuses to turn off her spiritual lights for the partner who is struggling through a personal storm of disconnectedness with God. Helen never stopped praying for her husband. She remained civil through the years of abandonment. She allowed grace to rule where bitterness may have seemed more" rational."

Through Alienation

For years Beth, a Christian wife, mourned the spiritual distance of her believing husband. He was aloof at home. Beth described a man whom his friends had never seen; publicly he was charming, upbeat, and fun.

"He can't be like that; Bill's so engaged in life," one friend said in disbelief.

"Yes," Beth explained, "that is the man I married. But privately, through the years, he has become emotionally unavailable. He avoids connecting with me, buries himself in his office at night, or avoids me in other ways. It's as if he's dug a moat around his heart and I no longer have a way to get in."

Beth heard the inner voices telling her, "You were made to be loved. You deserve better than this." However, she responded with determination; she held onto the ideal—discontent to settle for anything less than a real marriage, with a real relationship and real spiritual intimacy. For years, despite turning the light on Bill's emotional distance, (as opposed to sometimes simply *keeping* the lights on), nothing changed. Still they had many arguments. Finally, they had both had enough. After much pain and frustration, they agreed to see a marriage counselor.

Now, after a couple of years of counseling and recovery, they are enjoying a closeness they never had in the early years of their marriage. They are both dealing with their own issues—issues they would describe as spiritual ones, not simply marriage issues. But they are doing much better, as they experience the engaged, fully alive marriage God intended them to have. They have learned that they are made to be loved and that their marriage is the vehicle through which they will experience that love. Their friends now call them the "honeymooners" —Beth and Bill so enjoy being alone together that their friends find it difficult to get on the couple's social calendar.

This marriage is experiencing a "rebirthing" and is in process of becoming "as good as it can be." God does show up. But, until that time, someone must leave the lights on. Like Beth, we must be relentlessly hopeful, prayerful, and persistent.

Even Through Devastation

God is capable of healing even the most devastated marriages. Jeff's marriage failed after he was convicted and sent to prison. His wife,

Meg—like him, not a Christian—divorced him. But in prison Jeff accepted Christ as his personal Savior. After serving his term, he was released to a Christian halfway house. He began to attend church and experienced tremendous spiritual growth. In the midst of enormous life change, he felt compelled to reestablish his relationship with his wife.

At first Meg was reluctant, but eventually she realized that Jeff was a changed man. As her "ex" matured spiritually, she couldn't help but be drawn to his spiritual lights. The result? She too became a Christian, and to the great joy of all involved—the church, his housemates at the halfway house, their family and friends—they were eventually remarried.

These are wonderful stories, but we all know that sometimes marriage endings are not happy. "Keeping the lights on" can be emotionally exhausting—a long night season of the soul, full of anxious wondering, seemingly unfounded hoping, and suspicions that all our efforts are in vain. *Will it matter in the end? And furthermore, forget the future, how will I just get through today? Will God help us?*

BEWARE OF ANSWERED PRAYER

Yes, He will. His timing isn't always immediate, but when the answer comes, we should be ready.

Not long ago, I was reminded that God *does* hear our prayers and answers them. After this incident, I was also reminded anew that we must be careful what we pray because we may not, in actuality, be ready for certain prayers to be answered.

My summer project as the "artist in residence" at the Bell home was to furnish and decorate our front porch. For years a twig settee and matching armchairs with ticking pillows and faded black floral chintz have filled one end of our porch, along with angel statuaries that support our morning cups of coffee and plants and flowers. But one end of the porch had remained noticeably bare.

I was delighted when finally I found an old farm table at a garage sale. What a find! Its thick legs, painted black decades ago, now were cracked and faded. Perfect! Its top had been left its natural wood color, but was scarred and burned black in places. *Ah, character,* I told myself. *You can't buy that in a store.* It was love at first sight.

A Prayer for Feathers

I placed the table on our porch and decorated its top with plants and candles for nighttime enjoyment. I found some inexpensive tiny frames with black and ivory stripes and black and ivory dots and knew they were perfect companions to my table. I planned a nature museum. The frames would be displayed under the lip of the table, attached to the table's edge. Then I began to fill them: butterflies for the first two frames, tiny seashells and a miniature sand beach for the third, and birch bark and berries for the fourth. That left one empty frame. I knew what it needed. Feathers.

One morning while I was prayer-walking, my prayers kept coming back to this silly obsessive request about finding feathers to complete my table project. "God, it would just be so nice if, while I was walking this morning, I could find feathers for my frame." I walked for about thirty minutes and saw not one lousy feather. And then, before my eyes, lying ten yards ahead of me in the road, directly in my pathway, were feathers—an entire dead bird!

I walked up to it. Did I dare touch it? It looked buggy and repulsive. I didn't even want to nudge it with my shoe. But feathers seemed to be in short supply, my walk was almost over, and I *really* wanted to finish my project.

Did I ask for feathers—plural feathers—God? Really, did You think I could manage a whole dead bird? I reluctantly left the poor creature with all its feathers intact and walked back home. The closer to home, the more I wondered, *Should I have been more brave? Should I go back and pluck it?* But then, as I was walking up our driveway entertaining those thoughts, I saw it—one very small, perfect, unbuggy black feather, the exact size I needed for my frame.

Ahh, God! You're so funny. You just had to see how desperately I wanted a feather, didn't You? I bet You thought I'd go for that dead bird. Well, next time I'll be more careful about the exactitude of my prayers. And next time please have some pity on me and remember I can only manage so much blessing in my life!

How would you respond if God *really* answered your prayers about your spouse's spiritual condition? How many women pray a prayer about wanting a husband who is a man of God? But what would happen if your husband came home one night and announced that he was quitting his job and going to seminary? What if he suddenly decided to become a missionary to unreached tribes? How would you handle him marching into the front yard and staking a "For Sale" sign in the ground? Those kinds of life plans are not unusual for "men of God."

Would you be a woman who could handle *that* whole bird? Are you really prepared for God to answer such a prayer that would potentially greatly impact both of your lives?

Or what if the prayers of a husband for his wife to be more engaged in spiritual life with him were suddenly answered? Imagine the changes. Suddenly she is in church whenever the doors are opened, enrolling him in marriage seminars, trotting off to spiritual life conferences, planning family vacations around Christian conference schedules, wanting spiritual connectedness with him morning, noon, and night, pressing him for more indications of spiritual growth in his life, growing beyond him by leaps and bounds. A lot of spiritual women are like that.

Would he really be ready for *that* whole bird?

A Prayer for Deliverance

The wife of a workaholic prayed for years that God would heal her husband and bring him back into her life. All those years there was no change. She accepted the loneliness as her lot in life and made a life of her own. She vacationed alone or with other women friends. He never vacationed. She developed her own interests and professional life. She was a confidante to many other women and had close connections with many of them. Then, suddenly, without warning, her husband became convicted of his sin of workaholism. Now, for the first time in their long marriage, he was available and wanting to make up for the "years that the locust ate."

"I'm really struggling," she told us. "I have made an independent life without him. I have learned to enjoy it this way. Now he wants to be a 'together couple.' I am having to make some enormous adjustments and compensations in my life. I miss my independence. I had no idea what it would mean to have my prayers answered."

We grow impatient waiting for God to answer our prayers. "God help us. God help us *now!*" But perhaps there is a hidden mercy in our waiting. Perhaps we don't understand the full impact of the prayers we offer should they be answered. Instead of plural feathers, perhaps we should accept with joy one small feather from God, one small indication that there is a reason to hope, one small step towards shared spiritual intimacy, or one sign that even if nothing ever changes, we can bear it.

WHEN YOU RECEIVE ONLY A FEATHER

In our quest to remain the faithful spouse seeking after God, we will find at times only a partial answer, just one solitary feather. But that can be enough. It can assure us He is watching, that He is caring.

Jenny surely sought God's consolation as she watched her marriage breaking apart. Her husband had left her and their children, and he had turned from God into a life of selfishness and sinfulness. Even so, Jenny still loved him. Though she had suffered repeated betrayals and endured his lifestyle of promiscuity, she still wanted to try to make their marriage work. Then one day she wondered, *Am I crazy to still want him in my life?*

"Oh, God," Jenny prayed, "if You could just give me one indication of whether I should let him go or not. Could You somehow give me a sense of peace about where my heart should be directed?"

She turned to the Old Testament and came upon three verses that spoke to her:

"For I know the plans I have for you," declares the Lord, "plans to prosper you and not to harm you, plans to give you hope and a future. Then you will call upon me and come and pray to me, and I will listen to you. You will seek me and find me when you seek me with your whole heart. I will be found by you." (Jeremiah 29:11–13)

The verses were full of hope, but Jenny felt she dare not claim them as her own. With a heavy heart she attended church that Sunday still uncomforted and unsatisfied because she felt she could not presume upon God to speak so directly through Scripture.

She attended the second of three services. In the middle of the pastor's message he added as a side note these same verses from Jeremiah that she had read just that morning. *There they are again. Is it a coincidence?* Jenny asked herself. That evening she spoke to her pastor and mentioned the Jeremiah verses.

"Oh, interesting," the pastor responded. "Those verses were not a part of my original sermon. The only service where I felt led to share them was the service you attended."

Later Jenny asked our opinion. "Do you suppose that was a coincidence? Or should I cling to the hope of those verses as a gift that God actually gave to me?"

We said, "Pick up the feather, Jenny. It's yours. How many times does God have to answer your prayer with a message of love for you before you know it's yours to own? The answer to your prayer about where your heart should be directed is specific and clear. Direct your heart towards God and trust Him to meet all of your needs for your future."

Jenny's husband has not yet returned. To this day, she clings to the

Scripture passage as a promise from God to redirect her heart and trust Him to supply her needs for the days ahead.

Another woman is thrilled. Jill's husband has finally agreed to go to a Promise Keepers' stadium event, even though he told her that he thinks all this spiritual "male bonding" stuff is silly. "I can't sit in a bleacher seat all day praying and singing and trying to be interested in all those messages." But he went and she continued to pray that God would bring about significant change in her spiritually disinterested husband's life.

When he returned home, there was no apparent major change. He has not initiated family devotions. He's not yet taking any spiritual leadership. However, he is no longer negative about Promise Keepers. He had a great first-time experience and wants to go again.

It's a feather, Jill figures. Not the whole bird she's been praying for; but she can take encouragement that there is some progress in his spiritual openness. And she is right. God is at work.

Maybe a husband and wife will read this book together, but the only exercise the wife is willing to try is to start keeping an encouragement journal. Well, her growth may not be enormous—not exactly a renewed interest in Scripture and prayer—but it is something. Not the whole bird of spiritual renewal her husband prayed for, but it's an encouraging feather.

A lonely married heart goes to church and sings with the congregation:

> *O Love that wilt not let me go,*
> *I rest my weary soul in Thee;*
> *I give Thee back the life I owe,*
> *That in Thine ocean depths its flow*
> *May richer, fuller be.*
>
> *O Joy that seekest me through pain,*
> *I cannot close my heart to Thee;*
> *I trace the rainbow through the rain,*
> *And feel the promise is not vain*
> *That morn shall tearless be.*[2]

The words soothe and recycle like a love-stuck record in the lonely married's soul all day. "Were the words for me, God? Or am I presumptuous to claim this comfort as one personally given by You?"

It is a feather. It is even more than that. It is the lonely soul's feather to pick up and carry as a personal encouragement from God. God, who answers an obsessive woman's prayer about a silly feather, will surely not turn away from the more urgent prayers for spiritual intimacy and deep connectedness with our marriage partners. But while we wait, not knowing if our spouse will ever move towards God or towards us, God gives us "feathers" to direct our hearts back to Him.

KEEPING THE LIGHTS BURNING

God uses "feathers" to encourage us to keep our own spiritual lights burning for our own sakes, and for the sake of the one to whom we are married. A small prayer answered is an encouragement to keep the spiritual lights on, to keep praying, to keep loving even when we feel unsure any of it will change our situation.

"God, help us to receive the comfort You send us in order to experience Your love."

"God help us." We were made to be loved and in this fallen world we should count ourselves among the most fortunate of human beings if our married partner travels with us spiritually.

God will help us! Even though none of us can predict the endings of our own marriage stories, we have this certainty: God is for us and will never abandon us or turn from us.[3]

His lavish love is life's one surety. It is the fuel that fires our spiritual lights to keep burning for each other. May we all keep our spiritual lights burning brightly.

We leave you with this blessing:

May the day come when you and your spouse are able to enjoy the blessing of "the whole bird" of spiritual intimacy.

May your marriage be blessed with deep connectedness, spiritual satisfaction, joy in His presence, tender care for each other, and a growing mutual passion for God.

May your hearts well up in gratefulness to God with prayers inhabited by praise: "Thank You, God. You saved the best for last. This is wonderful stuff! Thank You for bringing and keeping us together."

Finally and most importantly, may you increasingly have the ability to hear and respond to God's voice as He personally tells you in His many resourceful, creative, and delightful ways: "You were *made to be loved*." And may your marriage be the human vehicle through which you give and receive that love.

Notes

Introduction

1. According to Bible commentators, the ephod extended to David's hips, encrusted with jewels representing the twelve tribes of Israel. Yet to Michal, David looked like anyone but a king. He had taken on the garment of a priest—a servant of God. Michal most likely objected to his public humbling of himself before God, to his inferior appearance (in removing his royal robes he had exposed his arms and legs to the people), and to his servile spiritual display.

Chapter 1: What Makes a Marriage Successful?

1. John W. Santrock, *Life-Span Development,* 6th ed. (Madison, Wisc.: Brown & Benchmark/McGraw-Hill, 1997), 455.

2. As quoted in John Bartlett, Justin Kaplan, gen. ed., *Familiar Quotations,* 16th ed. (Boston: Little, Brown, 1992), 347.

3. C. S. Lewis, as quoted in Wayne Martindale and Jerry Root, *The Quotable Lewis* (Wheaton, Ill.: Tyndale, 1989), 94.

Chapter 2: Made to Be Loved

1. Lawrence J. Crabb, Jr., *The Marriage Builder* (Grand Rapids: Zondervan, 1982), 10–11.

2. Dan Allender, *The Wounded Heart: Hope for Adult Victims of Childhood Sexual Abuse* (Colorado Springs: NavPress, 1990), 194–95.

Chapter 3: Where Is God?

1. William J. Petersen, *25 Surprising Marriages: Faith-Building Stories from the Lives of Famous Christians* (Grand Rapids: Baker, 1997), 252.
2. Samuel Beckett, *Waiting for Godot* (New York: Grove, 1954), 32.

Chapter 4: Longing for Intimacy

1. Joseph Scriven, "What a Friend We Have in Jesus." In public domain.
2. Elvina M. Hall, "Jesus Paid It All." In public domain.
3. Leon Morris, "I Corinthians," in *Tyndale New Testament Commentaries* (Downers Grove, Ill.: InterVarsity, 1958), 181; as quoted in David Prior, *The Message of I Corinthians* (Downers Grove, Ill.: InterVarsity, 1985), 226.
4. Henri Nouwen, *Life of the Beloved: Spiritual Living in a Secular World* (New York: Crossroad, 1996), 62–63.
5. J. Allen Petersen, *The Myth of the Greener Grass* (Wheaton: Tyndale, 1983), 63.
6. Dietrich Bonhoeffer, *Letters & Papers from Prison* (New York: Collier, 1953), 233–34.
7. David Wilkerson, *Have You Felt Like Giving Up Lately?* (Old Tappan, N.J.: Revell, 1980), 36.
8. Adapted from Neil T. Anderson, *Victory Over Darkness* (Ventura, Calif.: Regal, 1990), 45, 46.
9. C. S. Lewis, as quoted in Wayne Martindale and Jerry Root, *The Quotable Lewis* (Wheaton, Ill.: Tyndale, 1989), 411.
10. Henry T. Blackaby and Claude V. King, *Experiencing God* (Nashville: Broadman, 1994), 46.

Chapter 5: Called to Be Saints: Turning Houses into Homes

1. Frederick Buechner, *The Longing for Home* (New York: HarperCollins, 1996), 28.
2. C. S. Lewis, as quoted in Wayne Martindale and Jerry Root, *The Quotable Lewis* (Wheaton, Ill.: Tyndale, 1989), 420–21.

Chapter 6: The Rub: Counting the Cost

1. James Calvin Schaap, "Homecoming," *Christianity Today,* 1 September 1997, 28.
2. Thomas Moore, *Soul Mates: Honoring the Mysteries of Love and Relationship* (New York: HarperCollins, 1994), xvii.
3. Lawrence J. Crabb, Jr., *The Marriage Builder: A Blueprint for Couples and Counselors* (Grand Rapids: Zondervan, 1982), 124.

Chapter 7: Smoothing the Rub

1. Lawrence J. Crabb, Jr., *The Marriage Builder: A Blueprint for Couples and Counselors* (Grand Rapids: Zondervan, 1982), 140–41.
2. Bob Condor, "Uncovering the Secrets to Healthy Relationships," *Chicago Tribune,* 9 April 1998, sec. 5, p. 1.
3. Timmen Cermak, *A Time to Heal,* as quoted by Nancy Groom, *From Bondage to Bonding: Escaping Codependency, Embracing Biblical Love* (Colorado Springs: NavPress, 1991), 68.

4. Bruce Milne, *Know the Truth: A Handbook of Christian Belief* (Downers Grove, Ill.: Inter-Varsity, 1982), 70.

5. Oswald Chambers, *My Utmost for His Highest* (Grand Rapids: Discovery House, 1992), May 11.

Chapter 8: About Kings and Queens

1. Translated from the Irish epic poem, *Tain Bo Cuailnge, The Cattle Raid of Cooley,* as quoted in Thomas Cahill, *How the Irish Saved Civilization* (New York: Doubleday, 1995), 71–72.

2. Ibid., 72–73.

3. Anne Wilson Schaef, *Co-Dependence: Misunderstood, Mistreated,* as quoted in Nancy Groom, *From Bondage to Bonding: Escaping Codependency Embracing Biblical Love* (Colorado Springs: NavPress, 1991), 23.

4. Stephen E. Ambrose, *Undaunted Courage: Meriwether Lewis, Thomas Jefferson, and the Opening of the American West* (New York: Simon & Schuster, 1996), 285–86.

5. Ibid., 340.

6. David Stoop, *Experiencing God Together* (Wheaton, Ill.: Tyndale, 1996), 79.

7. Bruce Milne, *Know the Truth* (Downers Grove, Ill.: InterVarsity, 1982), 230.

8. Ibid., 231.

9. Larry Crabb, *Understanding People: Deep Longings for Relationship* (Grand Rapids: Zondervan, 1987), 102.

Chapter 9: When Things Spiritual Seem Dull

1. Oswald Chambers, *My Utmost for His Highest* (Grand Rapids: Discovery House, 1992), May 12.

2. Bruce Milne, *Know the Truth: A Handbook of Christian Belief* (Downers Grove, Ill.: Inter-Varsity, 1982), 230.

3. As quoted in Hugh C. Warner, *Daily Readings from William Temple* (London: Hodder & Stoughton, 1948), 29.

4. You can enhance a prayer walk with appropriate cassette music. Valerie has produced an effective audiocassette, "PrayerWalk: Care for Body and Soul," which includes music and guided prayer topics. In addition, she has two other prayer walk tapes: "Prayer-Walk II" and "Classic PrayerWalk: Blessing Your Community." For information on obtaining these tapes and other resources by the Bells, see page 215.

5. "Give Thanks" by Henry Smith, © 1978 Integrity's Hosanna! Music/ASCAP. All rights reserved. International copyright secured. Used by permission.

6. David Mains and Steve Bell, *Two Are Better Than One: A Guide to Prayer Partnerships That Work* (Shippenburg, Pa. Destray Image, 1995) This book is also available directly from the author. See page 215.

Chapter 10: Sexuality and the Spiritually Intimate Marriage

1. Lawrence J. Crabb, Jr., *The Marriage Builder: A Blueprint for Couples and Counselors* (Grand Rapids: Zondervan, 1982), 91–92.

2. Stanton L. Jones, as quoted in Ron R. Lee, *The Marriage You've Always Wanted* (Colorado Springs: Victor, 1997), 94–95.

3. The phrases *users of passion, abusers of passion,* and *dulled to passion* come from Dan Allender, *The Wounded Heart* (Colorado Springs: NavPress, 1990), 247.

4. Judith Couchman, *A Garden's Promise: Spiritual Reflections on Growing from the Heart* (Colorado Springs: Waterbrook Press, 1997), 81.

5. Allender, *The Wounded Heart,* 165. For further reading on sexual dysfunction in this area we suggest *The Wounded Healer* by Dan Allender, which deals with sexual dysfunction within the framework of childhood sexual abuse but has pertinent information for any couple struggling with sexual dysfunction regardless of whether there is a history of sexual abuse.

Chapter 11: Just Don't Ask Me to Pray!

1. Frederick Buechner, *Listening to Your Life* (San Francisco: HarperCollins, 1992), 211–12.

2. Douglas J. Rumford, *Soul Shaping: Taking Care of Your Spiritual Life* (Wheaton, Ill.: Tyndale, 1996), 97–98.

3. Jan Johnson, *Enjoying the Presence of God* (Colorado Springs: NavPress, 1996), 11.

4. Walter Wangerin, Jr., *Whole Prayer: Speaking and Listening to God* (Grand Rapids: Zondervan, 1998), 95–96.

Chapter 12: Leaving the Lights On

1. Gerald May as quoted in Luci Shaw, *Water My Soul: Cultivating the Interior Life* (Grand Rapids: Zondervan, 1998), 121.

2. George Matheson, "O Love That Will Not Let Me Go." In public domain.

3. See especially the Scripures' promise in Romans 8:32, 35–39 and Hebrews 13:5b.

If you are interested in contacting Steve or Valerie Bell about speaking at your church, organization, or special event, write or call at:

Steve or Valerie Bell
P.O. Box 1399
Wheaton, IL 60189
Phone/Fax 630-668-8412

To learn about other books by the Bells, as well as audio and video-tape resources, please write or call at the above address.